Given Away

Olan Hill Jr.

Author's Tranquility Press
ATLANTA, GEORGIA

Olan Hill Jr. /Author's Tranquility Press
3800 Camp Creek Pkwy SW Bldg. 1400-116 #1255
Atlanta, GA 30331, USA
www.authorstranquilitypress.com

Ordering Information:
Quantity sales. Special discounts are available on quantity purchases by corporations, associations, and others. For details, contact the "Special Sales Department" at the address above.

Given Away/Olan Hill Jr.
Paperback: 978-1-961908-99-4
eBook: 978-1-962492-00-3

Table of Contents

Dedication

*To my wonderful wife, Mary Lou, for her unfailing love and support.

*To my children and their spouses, Holli (Marvin), Doyle, Chuck (Lori) for always believing in me.

*To my grandchildren & their spouses, Heidi (Steve), Heather, Hanna (Jonathan), Harrison, Jonathan, Savannah, Preston, & Carson.

And to my great grandchildren, JerriLynn, Joslyn, Javin, Katie, & Jaxson.

May this story inspire you to live life to its fullest.

*To my church family, Pleasant Grove Assembly of God who encouraged me to write my story.

*And above all, I dedicate this book...

To my heavenly Father, who loved me, cared for me, rescued me, and gave me hope for tomorrow.

Introduction

Given Away

I T WAS ONE of those cool October days in California. The wind was slowly bringing the chilled air down from the nearby mountains. October in central California can be bleak and even depressing at times. I was about to find out just how depressing things could become.

On that October day in 1947, I was barely nine years old. Walking home from school, I turned into the little house where my family lived. As I did, I found all my belongings (clothes, shoes, and everything I owned), carefully packed in a small cardboard box. The box was sitting on the front porch of that little clapboard house where we lived, in Bean Town (just outside Clovis, California). Climbing the steps that day, my mind spun with curiosity. Immediately, the front door opened, and my stepmother confronted me with a sinister smile on her face.

Shocked and perplexed I asked, "Why are my things out here?" I will never forget her answer. "Your Daddy has given you away!" she exclaimed.

Given me away? I wondered what those words could possibly mean. You can't just give someone away, can you? But her words that day came true. My daddy had given me away to a man I did not know, to be taken to a place I had never been, to be raised as he saw fit.

My worst fears had come true. In one fell swoop I experienced a total rejection from my father as he gave me away.

Is that possible? Could he do that? Oh Yes! He could and he did! On that day, I was given me away?

Charles, Mary and me at the Okmulgee Ice House.

CHAPTER 1

The Beginning

DURING THE DAYS of the Great Depression, the American dream had all but vanished and was replaced with a deep sense of hopelessness. People who had once believed they lived in the land of opportunity, witnessed those opportunities fade into the past like the morning dew. Their greatest aspirations had all but transformed into difficult days of sorrow and desperation. What had once been a time of hope and optimism had shifted to a time of despair.

By 1931, the rains had stopped and the powerful dust storms carrying millions of tons of sand, swept across Oklahoma. As the rains disappeared, the crops withered and died. The land (forced to live on little water) quickly became parched. The harsh winds blew strong and pounded against everything in its path. So began the dry and depressing days of the dust storms that blew ruthlessly across the nation's heartland. My grandparents were farmers and all they knew to do was plow the ground, plant seed, and hope for rain. It was a desperate time for poor people living in Oklahoma.

In writing this book of my beginnings, I simply want to tell my story. As I look back on my life and the journey I have come, I'm grateful for God's abiding presence and faithful care. It is with a clear heart and with no sense of blame that I pen these words. There will be stories which will be more difficult to write and some that may not be flattering or complimentary in their nature. However, it is my intention to simply tell my story and to reveal the way my Father in Heaven has always watched over me during the good days and the bad. So, I have no one to blame, and I don't write with anger, hate, or even sorrow. I only want to tell my story as I saw it, good, bad, or indifferent.

My story begins with a man named Oliver Duckworth. Oliver was my paternal grandfather who was at that time living in Arkansas with his wife Sarah McAnnelly and their three children (Oliver Jr, Bertha, and my mother Etta Mae). Grandpa Duckworth was a strong man with a strong family lineage. He had the privilege of being born into a family of pioneers deep in the Ozark Mountains of Arkansas. His father had lived there all his life. In fact, he had worked to clear his own land and built his house with his own hands – but those days were gone. The land grant of 60 acres was gone and times had changed. The land was not able to provide for Grandpa's large family, so he felt it was time to sell and move on.

Grandpa "Duck" (as we knew him) and Grandma Sarah had married in Fort Smith, Arkansas on August 4, 1915. At that time, he was twenty-two and she was sixteen (a common occurrence during those days). Grandpa, like most hard-working people in the early nineteen hundreds, was a poor man with little or no education. He worked hard and did his best to provide for the family, but over the next few years the opportunity for work became scarce, which made feeding his family very difficult. Even though Grandpa Duck worked from sunup to sundown, his labor never seemed to be enough.

During those days, Grandma Sarah grew constantly dissatisfied with their marriage. The financial strain and burden of bills added enormous pressure to their relationship. There was never enough money for the things she wanted. As the days continued, the belief that her life was passing her by continued to grow. After several more years she decided she just didn't want to be married or have that life any longer. With an increasing feeling that her life would be improved far away from Arkansas and those days of meager earnings, she packed up what little belongings she had and headed for Texas. In doing so, she was leaving Grandpa Duck alone to care for their three children.

The belief that she could leave her past behind and start another life far away had consumed her. However, she never found the life she was looking for. Things in Texas proved to be just as difficult as things in Arkansas. And even though she lived a long life, she never married again—spending the rest of her life living alone. At the time of her death, she occupied a very small house in Oklahoma near her brother, Marion.

Mama and my wife Mary Lou attended her funeral and even stayed a few days wrapping up loose ends and taking care of what little business she had left behind.

One of the few things she owned was the little house she died in. Since Mama was her nearest kin, she inherited the little house, and was forced to dispose of it. To say it was small would be an understatement. It was barely large enough for one person to live in. In total, it had one little bedroom, a small bathroom, and a living area (consisting of a tiny kitchen with a small apartment size stove).

Mama decided to give the house to the church my grandma had been attending. She and Mary Lou set about cleaning it before turning it over to the church. Mama's Uncle Marion had told her that Grandma wanted her to know about her savings. He added that my grandma wanted him to relay the importance of looking under that tiny kitchen stove. So, before the place was given away, my great Uncle Marion disconnected the stove and pulled it out from the wall. There, to everyone's surprise, were hidden several bank envelopes containing various amounts of cash. For several years grandma had been cashing her social security check as soon as it arrived. After paying any bills she may have owed, she would then put the rest of the money under her stove for safekeeping. Grandma obviously didn't trust banks, so she had saved her money and hid it under the stove. Mama, Mary Lou and Uncle Marion spent the next several hours emptying the envelopes and counting the money inside. When it was all counted, it amounted to several thousand dollars. Though it must have seemed like a small treasure, I can't help but wonder what treasures Grandma missed out on by leaving her family and children many years earlier.

Sometime after Grandma Duckworth moved to Texas, Grandpa Duck filed for divorce. After a few years he married again. He had several more children with his new wife. In the fall of 1932, Grandpa Duck moved with all his children to the little town of Okmulgee, Oklahoma. It was there that he found a job, rented a house, and settled down with his new wife and family.

My paternal grandma, Gertrude Smith, also lived in Arkansas with her five sisters and one brother. During the early nineteen hundreds, she and her family moved from Arkansas to Oklahoma as well.

Her father was John Smith, and her mother was a precious woman named Sarah. Sarah was part Creek Indian and had settled in the town of Okmulgee some years earlier. Gertrude Smith, my grandmother was said to have married a man by the name of Jasper Hill, a traveling salesman. Not much is known of Jasper. Supposedly, he traveled through the state of Arkansas, selling his pots and pans to anyone he could. According to the "hush-hush rumors," Jasper supposedly married my grandma Gertrude after she became pregnant with her first child, Doyle. Following the so-called marriage, Jasper Hill continued his way selling pots and pans.

As the story goes, he would return from time to time for a visit, just long enough to father another child. During those ensuing years, Grandma had four children: Doyle, Olan Sr., Edith, & Bonnie. Jasper Hill finally disappeared after several years and was never heard from again. No one really knows what happened to him (or if he really even existed).

While living at home with her mother and father in Okmulgee, Oklahoma, my grandma met and married a loving and caring man named Wes Petree. Together they reared their family and remained married for 60 years. Wes Petree was the only paternal grandpa I ever knew, but I knew he loved my siblings and me and treated us as if we were his own grandchildren.

Now, while this story was the official version of the beginning of the Hill family, there is another story, which has only been told in bits and pieces and shadowed moments over the years. The story to which I am referring is a very different one from that one stated above. It tells a very different experience for my Grandma Gertrude. According to the unofficial version of our history, my grandma was never really married to anyone named Jasper Hill. How the name Jasper Hill came into our family, is anyone's guess, because no one ever met him or knew of his existence before the family moved to Oklahoma.

Our family can only trace its existence back to my grandma's father, John Smith who is said to have himself fathered all four of her children. Since DNA mapping had not been discovered in those days, no one knows for sure which story is true. I'm not convinced that it really matters anyway—because the only ones who could reveal the details of what really happened in those days are dead and gone, and with them the truth as well.

Grandma and Grandpa Petree

CHAPTER 2
Grandma Petree

WHEN I WAS a little boy there were not too many people on whom I could depend. My Mama and Daddy had divorced; my brother and sister were living with other family members. I had been sent to live with my Grandma Petree in Okmulgee, Oklahoma. I was full of mischief and hard to handle, but somehow Grandma, was able to keep me in check.

Grandma was very meticulous about her personal care. Before she ever showed herself in the morning, she made sure her hair was always perfect, and would never let anyone see any gray. She kept it died jet black, long, braided, and swept up on the top of her head. She always had a clean starched dress with a clean starched white apron that she changed every day.

Her one vice was snuff. For those who may not be familiar with snuff, it is a dried powdery form of tobacco. As long as she lived, she dipped snuff. You almost never saw it because she was always careful not to let it show, but she always had some between her cheek and jaw. She carried a spit can with her everywhere she went and again, was careful not to let anyone see her spit. Her snuff came in glass containers, and when they were empty, she would wash them out and use them for glasses.

Grandma was a very loving woman, and she had a giving heart. Whenever someone visited her, she wanted to give them something to take back home with them. Sometimes it would be one of her jars of canned food or sometimes one of her homemade quilts, or just whatever she had to offer. If she didn't have anything better to give, she would give away a set of her snuff glasses.

On one of our trips to Oklahoma she gave Mary Lou, my wife, an antique tobacco stand, lined with copper that my Daddy and Mama had purchased many years before in the days before their divorce. It remains in my family as one of the few items from my daddy and mama's years together.

I always loved going to Grandma's house. It wasn't much, but it was always well cared for. The truth is it was always spotless. Her linoleum floors were always swept and mopped (a ritual she performed several times a day). Her walls and furniture were decorated with family photos, and sparkling mottos of Jesus that she received from buying cans of Cloverine salve from traveling salesmen. I guess she had a thing for traveling salesmen. She displayed everything that was given to her, in one way or another. You could always find your own picture on display among the many she kept placed all over the house. She kept a large feather mattress on top of her bed, and whenever anyone came to stay overnight, she would take it off her bed and put it on the living room floor, for her guests to sleep on. I still recall the feel of that old feather bed, and her homemade quilts piled on top for cover.

Looking back now, I think Grandma Petree was the only person I could depend on, and the only one who really loved me, at least in an unconditional way. There were no strings attached to Grandma's love. I didn't have to do anything to earn it because she just loved me.

Over the years I've learned that there are different kinds of love people offer. Some people will love you with an "If" attached. If you are good, or if you do something for them, or if you give them something they want—they will love you. Then, there are those who love you "Because." Because you do something, or because you don't do something, or because they want something, or because of this or that they love you. But Grandma Petree never attached and "If" or a "Because" to her love. She just loved me because she was my Grandma.

I have learned over the years; grandmas are like that. Grandma Petree had a quilting rack that hung from the ceiling, by a pulley and a rope. When she had time to quilt, she would let it down and quilt for a while, then pull it back up to the ceiling until later. Using this method, she would make several quilts a year.

Every Sunday Grandma cooked dinner for the family. It was always a feast. She always had fried chicken, mashed potatoes/gravy, green beans, sliced tomatoes, cucumbers and onions, and a huge pan of cornbread. She did her own canning and stored everything in a storm cellar out back of the house, where we were made to go and wait if bad weather was in the area. Our storm cellar was built near the house and could only accommodate our family. It was only about ten by twelve feet, and an arched roof that would keep the water and wind out until the storm was over. It was entirely underground and gave us protection from tornadoes, which were so common in Oklahoma.

Grandma kept her onions tied to the ceiling on her back porch and when she wanted an onion, she went out on the porch and pulled one down from the ceiling. Those onions came in handy one day when I got in trouble with her, and she took after me with a broom. As I ran out the back door and down the porch, I reached up and grabbed one of those onions and ran out into the backyard. When she opened the screen door on the back porch waving her broom, I turned and let her have it with that onion. I knew she could not run as fast as I could, so I thought I didn't have to worry.

What I didn't know was about the same time we were having our little problem my Aunt Bonnie Dean came to visit. When I fired on Grandma with that onion and turned to run, my Aunt Bonnie took off after me. For a girl, she could really run and after about a block she caught me. She whipped me all the way back home. With every step we took, she took a swing at my backside. I thought she was going to kill me, but the only thing injured was my pride. My pride was hurt for letting a girl out run me!

Grandma and Grandpa had a special love for each other. The older they got the more affection they showed. Grandpa would often tease Grandma calling her "Gertie" and she loved it! Even though it was hard to get her riled up, she could become like a lion when her grandkids were in trouble. Once when we were living in California, she came by our house to visit and discovered our stepmother had sent us to bed without anything to eat. She told us to get up and she was going to cook something for us to eat. I was so scared, not knowing which one to obey. I also figured that when my Grandma left, my stepmother would punish us even more. Beatings were common and I had learned to put cardboard in my underwear so the beatings would not hurt so much. I can't remember if we got a whipping after she left or not, but I was so hungry I didn't care.

I don't remember my Grandma ever going to church, but I knew Grandma was proud of me. She seemed to be very happy when I told her I was a pastor in Florida. Grandma often read her bible and watched her favorite TV preacher (Oral Roberts), on TV every Sunday.

My Grandma died in 1990 at the age of ninety-eight. The one regret I still live with today is that I couldn't return to Oklahoma to attend her funeral. I truly loved Grandma and thank God for putting her in my life!

Mom and Dad 1944

CHAPTER 3
Etta and Olan

IN 1933 ETTA Mae Duckworth, my mother, married my Daddy, Olan Hill, in the little town of Okmulgee, Oklahoma. Since Daddy had quit school in the third grade to go to work in the fields to help support the family, he was unable to get a very good job; however, he did manage to find work at the local ice plant. For the first few years of their marriage things went pretty well. Daddy delivered ice to the people of Okmulgee in the morning and would return to the icehouse to make ice for the next day's run. Daddy and Mama lived in a small house on the edge of Okmulgee, where three children were born into the family, Charles, Mary Ellen, and me. Mama stayed home and took care of their children. Even though the depression was said to be over, someone forgot to tell my family because we were still depressed. There never seemed to be enough money to make ends meet in our household, and Mama and Daddy were always fighting over something. Money was always a good topic to use to start a fight, or sometimes it was over Daddy's drinking and womanizing.

Once when he came home from work, he had a brand-new pair of shoes that he said he intended to wear to a dance that night in Okmulgee. When he went to take his bath, Mama turned on the oven and placed his brand-new shoes in it and waited. After he got dressed and ready to go out he asked my Mama where she had put his shoes. She pointed to the oven, and as he ran to take them out, he discovered they were well done. The toe and the heel had curled up and were almost touching! I don't think he went dancing that night. Oh! What a fight.

Once when they got into an argument at the dinner table, Mama got so mad that when he reached for something, she stuck a fork clear through his hand and into the table. They both had quick tempers and would fight at the drop of a hat. I thought we had a normal family and that everyone fought like that.

In 1939, my Daddy heard that things were good in California, and that work was plentiful. So, they decided to pack up, leave Oklahoma and head for California. He quit his job, loaded all his worldly possessions into a Model A Ford and headed for the west.

My mother's sister, Bertha had married and moved to the town of Oildale, near Bakersfield, California. Mama and Daddy settled in the little valley town of Bakersfield, in order to be near her sister. Work was plentiful and Daddy soon got a job in the oil fields. While the family was doing well financially, the marriage itself was coming apart. Daddy started drinking, gambling, staying out late, and running around with other women while everyday Mama got more and more fed up. One day, she announced she had had enough of his lifestyle and was leaving. She moved out of our little house and moved in with her sister Bertha. Mama got a job as a waitress and soon was able to find a place of her own.

Daddy on the other hand had three children to take care of while trying to work and earn a living. It was not easy to provide for his children and work at the same time. He decided the best thing for him to do would be to return to Oklahoma where he would have help from his family with his kids. He again loaded up his Model A Ford, and headed back to Okmulgee, taking his three kids with him. When we got back to Okmulgee, Daddy got his old job back at the ice plant. Once again, he was back delivering ice in the morning, and working at the plant, making ice in the afternoon, for the next day's run.

*Living in a tent in Jimmy's Camp. Charles, Mary, Donna &
me.*

CHAPTER 4
Living with Family

DADDY SENT CHARLES and Mary Ellen to live with his brother, Doyle, and his wife Oleta, who lived in Okemah. I went to live with his sister, Edith, and her husband, Pat Sitten. At the time Aunt Edith and Uncle Pat had no children of their own (they later had a boy "James") so thankfully they were happy to take me in. Somewhere along the line they began to call me "Peewee", I guess it was because I was so little. As I grew older, I changed my name to "Pete". I wondered when I later became a principal, how it would have sounded to be introduced to the school board as "Mr. Peewee Hill!"

Uncle Doyle had purchased some ranchland, just north of Henrietta Oklahoma. I guess because they had no children of their own, and they had this large ranch they were willing to take in Charles and Mary Ellen. Uncle Doyle had worked in the oil fields in Oklahoma City and saved enough money to buy 200 acres of land, with a house, between Okemah and Henrietta. While my brother and sister were living with Uncle Doyle and Aunt Oleta, I spent my time living between my aunts Edith and Bonnie Dean, Daddy's two sisters.

During the time I was living with Uncle Pat and Aunt Edith, Uncle Pat got kicked in his side by a horse, and soon after, he died of his injuries. It was an awful time for Aunt Edith and her young son James. She had to give up the farm and move back in with Grandma.

A short time after Uncle Pat's death, I was sent to live with Uncle Doyle and Aunt Oleta. For the first time in several years all three of us kids were living together. Uncle Doyle's wife, Aunt Oleta was only sixteen when she married Uncle Doyle, but she was a good wife and loved him until the day he died.

Since she and Uncle Doyle didn't have any children of their own, they took us in and cared for us at different times through the years. They were good to us and tried to make us feel loved and wanted. They even bought us a horse named "Ribbon", which we learned to ride. It was great fun living on the ranch with Uncle Doyle and Aunt Oleta. There was a huge gully running across the back of his ranch and we loved to go there and play Cowboys and Indians for hours on end.

Once while we were running and shooting with our BB guns, Charles shot me right between the eyes. The BB stuck just under the skin and when, Aunt Oleta saw it, she threatened him with the whipping of his life if he ever shot at me again with that BB gun.

On another occasion Charles and our cousin Sammy were playing the good guys and bad guys and I was supposed to be the bad guy. They caught me, tied my hands behind my back, and proceeded to hang me. They brought a wooden box and made me stand on it while they threw the rope over a limb and tied it off. They put the rope around my neck and kicked the box out from under me and took off to hide. Aunt Oleta was washing clothes and came out to hang her clothes, about the same time I was hung. She screamed and ran over to me and lifted me up and took the rope off. I don't know how long I hung there, but I'm sure I wouldn't be writing this story if she had been a few minutes later.

Charles was a great brother and was the type of person who could learn anything if given a little time. Even though he never had the opportunity to go to college, he was much smarter than most college graduates. He could do almost anything on the construction line. He could pick up a 2X8 and turn it on its side and tell you if it was good to use or should be thrown back on the woodpile.

I called him back in the seventies and asked if he would be able to give me three weeks during that summer to build a house in North Carolina. He said he could, so I ordered all the lumber for the house, from a floor plan at 84 Lumber.

When the materials were delivered to the site, there were 2x4s, 2x8s, flooring, siding, and roofing, everything you needed to build a house. It just looked like a pile of lumber to me, but Charlie looked at it and saw a house.

Charlie and Albert Martin, my good friend, arrived at the site a week before me, and had everything lain out by the time I got there. I thought there is no way we will be able to get this house built in three weeks. But three weeks later we had three bedrooms, two baths, the house completely dried in, and ready to finish on the inside. Charlie was a building genius.

While building our house, Charlie was the construction ramrod and told everyone what to do. Not only did he oversee that the house was built, but he saw to it that everything was done properly. He had the patience of Job. He would say to me "build this door frame", and then show me how to do it. When I finished, he would say, "Now tear that out and do it the way I told you". After about the third time, he would say, "Now that's right". There was almost nothing he couldn't do when it came to building.

When Uncle Doyle purchased his ranch back in the early forties, he didn't know they would discover oil on the property. To his surprise he hadn't purchased the mineral rights, so all the oil that was pumped out went to the Oklahoma Oil Co. They did, however, give him the use of any gas he could capture before it was dispersed in the atmosphere. We were one of the few people in the area who had gaslights throughout our house.

Uncle Doyle also discovered how to use drip gasoline from the leaks in the oil well pipelines. It was not refined but it would run in his old model A Ford, and since gasoline was fifteen cents a gallon, it was a big saving. Though they never went to church, Uncle Doyle and Aunt Oleta were both God fearing people and would help anyone in need whenever they could. They were poor and ignorant in many ways, but wise in others. They gave us the best they had, and I will always be grateful for their love and care during my early years. Daddy rented a small house in Okmulgee at "808 North Sherman" and lived there while working at the ice plant.

On weekends and holidays, we would go to Okmulgee and stay with Grandma Petree so we could be near daddy. It was while we visited Grandma Petree that we got our first taste of church. Grandma's sister, Aunt Bonnie Ansiel, was a Christian woman and took us to church whenever possible. It was during this time Aunt Bonnie took us to a little Pentecostal Church of God in Okmulgee, which was my first introduction to Pentecost.

Long after becoming an adult, I thought the reason it was called "Pentecostal" was because it cost us pennies every time we would go to church. Grandma Petree or Aunt Bonnie would give us pennies to put in the offering, thus the name "Penny Costal!"

About a year after moving back to Oklahoma, Daddy decided to get a divorce. He filed for divorce in the Okmulgee courthouse, citing Mama for abandoning her children and since she lived in California, she didn't contest it.

Several years later Mama married a navy veteran, named Philip Berch, in a civil ceremony in Bakersfield, California. Phil was Catholic and wanted to be married in the church, but the Catholic Church would not grant it, because both he and Mama had been divorced. The only way he could have a church sanctioned marriage was to have their first marriages annulled.

I don't know how Phil got his annulled, but Mama came up with a great plan. According to her, she was never legally married to Daddy in the first place but was sold at auction to my Daddy when she was only nineteen. Actually, she said to me,

"Olan, paid my father one hundred dollars for me." I don't know where my Daddy would have gotten that kind of money, because up until that time in his life, he probably had never seen a hundred dollars. Be that as it may, she stuck to her story and applied to the church to have her marriage annulled.

In order to verify her story, the church sent a priest to Oklahoma to interview her family and friends, asking them to confirm her story. Of course, no one had ever heard that story and it took many interviews before someone was found to agree with it. That's all it took for her to get her annulment (that, and several hundred dollars). Now she was able to get married in the Catholic Church. Soon after, she joined the church and became an active member for the rest of her life. Their daughter, (my half-sister) Connie, even joined a convent in New York City and spent several months in training to become a nun.

Years later, I had an opportunity to ask Mama about the annulment, and she told me that it was true. She insisted my Daddy had paid her father one hundred dollars for her. I said to her "Mama since you were not married to Daddy, do you know what that makes me?" She never responded.

Dad's second family

Donna, Bertha, Jimmy, David, & Barbara

CHAPTER 5
Daddy's Second Marriage

WHEN I WAS five years old, Daddy married a young teen age girl from Okmulgee, Oklahoma who was pregnant, named Beulah. Beulah had told him the baby was his, and he felt obligated to "do the right thing", so they were married in the Okmulgee courthouse.

Some years later Beulah told him the little girl, Donna Sue, wasn't his at all, but she had only told him she was at the time so he would marry her. To his credit Daddy never let anyone know that Donna Sue wasn't his. I never knew the whole story until I was grown. He raised her and loved her as if she was truly his own. I think he really believed Donna Sue was his daughter, and Beulah may have only told him Donna wasn't his, just for spite. Daddy needed someone to take care of his children and Beulah needed a husband so, they were married and moved into the little house in Okmulgee, on Sherman Avenue.

Soon after the marriage, he gathered up his three children from Uncle Doyle and moved us into the house with his new wife. From the very beginning the marriage was rocky. Beulah was only sixteen years old and suddenly the mother of three children, pregnant, with a husband and family. It was just too much for a young girl to handle.

After being married about a year Daddy decided it was time to return to California. He packed everything we had in his old Model "A" including a mattress on top of everything in the back where we kids rode. We kids rode on top of a mattress about ten inches between all our stuff, and the oilcloth top of that old car. It was hard to turn over and there was no way to sit up at all, but somehow, we managed. I'm sure we looked like the "Clampetts" from the TV series "The Beverly Hillbillies". The heat wasn't too bad in Oklahoma, but when we reached the deserts of Nevada and California, it was well over 100 degrees. I can't imagine why we didn't die from the heat.

We traveled old Route 66 from Oklahoma City, to Bakersfield California. It was a two-lane road paved most of the way, but was in much need of repair, with potholes and washouts all along the way. It was not a straight road to California, but intentionally weaved its way through many small towns from Oklahoma to California. US 66 was the road of choice when traveling from the Midwest to the West. John Steinbeck called it the "mother road". All along the way, you could see all manner of roadside attractions from teepee shaped motels to Indian curio shops to reptile farms.

I guess Daddy didn't have much money because we only stopped for gas and bread and what few groceries Beulah could cook on an open fire. I had heard a story about money growing on trees. I really believed it did and I could not wait to get to California so I could go out and pick $5's and $10's and maybe a $50 or even a $100 now and then.

We drove during the day and would pull over beside the road at night and set up a camp. We had a tent for Daddy and Beulah to sleep in and we kids made our bed in the front seat of the car or on the ground next to it. We heard about people getting robbed and killed, so Daddy kept a loaded shotgun with him all the time.

At night Daddy would gather up some wood and build a fire and Beulah would get out the pots and pans and start supper. We carried a cloth bag on the front of the car filled with water and we used it for drinking, cooking and to fill the radiator when it got dry.

Some might think it strange that people traveled like that, but there were a lot of other families going to California in the same way we were. You could see all types of transportation from cars to trucks piled high with everything they could carry. There were many cars stopped along the road for one reason or another. They all had the same dream; if they could just get to California things would be better. We had a few problems along the way. The radiators would overheat, and we would have to find water to fill it and that was not easy, especially out in the desert. A tire would blow out and we would have to find a tube. Sometimes Daddy would hitchhike into the nearest town to patch a tube or buy a new one and then hitchhike back, put it on the car, and take off again.

Somewhere near Clovis, New Mexico we broke a rear axle. With no money and no way to get another one we pushed the car over beside a sign advertising Bull Durham smoking tobacco. Daddy took a blanket and nailed it up to one side of the sign, which was about six feet off the ground, and then he nailed up another one on the other side to create a type of tent. He unloaded the car then put most of our stuff under the makeshift tent. After getting the camp set up, he set out hitchhiking to the nearest town to wire Uncle Doyle and ask him for help.

When Uncle Doyle received the telegram, he agreed to join us and go to California. He had a small ranch near Okemah, Oklahoma. So before leaving he had to take care of the business, such as sell all his livestock, buy an axel for our old car, and make what other preparations he had to make. After that he had to load his old truck with all his and Aunt Oleta's things, and head out to find us.

Meanwhile, we kids were having the time of our lives. I saw my first horned toad out there in the desert and for the next couple of weeks we built ditches and arenas and played with the toads. From time-to-time people would stop and camp near us and we would play with other children who were also on their way to California. People from Oklahoma, Arkansas, and Texas were all trying to find a better life.

When I first saw the movie "The Grapes of Wrath", it was like seeing a replay of my own life, and our trip to California. After about two weeks Uncle Doyle and Aunt Oleta pulled off the road to our little camp with our new axel and wow! Were we ever glad to see them. Daddy was a pretty good mechanic, and it only took him about a day to remove the old broken axle and replace it with a new one. From then on, we traveled together. Sometimes we kids would take turns riding with Uncle Doyle and Aunt Oleta. It was always more fun to ride with them.

Crossing the desert was great fun for Charles, Mary, and me. There was the Painted Desert, and old Route 66 ran right threw it. It looked like a rainbow off in the distance and I still remember it today. The Painted Desert is in Arizona and stretches from the Grand Canyon to the Petrified Forest just north of the Little Colorado River. Millions of years ago huge trees grew there. Over the years many of these trees fell and were washed into the ground. Over millions of years the forces of erosion slowly brought the petrified wood to the surface, with trees as hard as stone. You could still see the rings in the wood, which are millions of years old.

I actually have one of those petrified pieces of wood that I picked up years later, when I took Mary Lou to California. We now use it as a doorstep. Most of the area that we call the Petrified Forest is protected as the Petrified Forest National Wilderness Park and is in the Navajo Nation.

The Navajo and the Hopi Indians have lived there for over a thousand years. Also, there were the cliff dwellers; homes build by Indians in the side of the mountains. All the cliff dwellers lived in northern Arizona. All along the way there would be Indians of different tribes, including the Pueblo, Navajo, Hopi and even some Apache, selling their baskets and beads along the roadsides.

Sometimes at night the desert would get down as low as freezing and then get up into the 100's in the daytime. The most challenging part of the trip was going over the mountains. Daddy's old car would barely crawl up the steep road, but somehow it made it.

Mom and Dad on their way to California with Charles and me.

CHAPTER 6

California

EVEN THOUGH THINGS were hard and money was scarce, as children we didn't know we were poor or even in need. Everyone we knew was more or less like we were. It wasn't unusual to go hungry, but we knew we wouldn't starve, we knew Daddy would make a way somehow, so it was never a worry for us. We knew if we could just get to California where money grew on trees, we would be all right.

After weeks on the road, we finally arrived in California. We ended our trip in a makeshift camp called Weed Patch. This camp was built by the government to take care of people like us, coming from Oklahoma, and the Midwest. These were desperate times, and many of the "Okies" were exploited and abused.

People had very little money, so they were willing to work in the fields just to get enough food to feed their families. Often the farm owners let us get supplies from their own store. At the end of the week, they would keep most of our wages for whatever we owed. It always cost much more at their store than it did in town, but no store would give us credit in town.

The camps were not all bad. Most of the people who lived in these camps were from Oklahoma or Arkansas and it was sort of like being back home with the people we knew. There was always a lot of hostility toward "Okie's"; the locals didn't want their kids going to school with us. But that was ok because it gave us more time to work in the fields.

Cutting grapes was hard work and it was always hot. Most of the grapes in the valley were harvested in July and August. In order to cut the grapes, you had to go up under the vines to find them, and you had to watch out for wasp nests. There were always plenty of wasps up under the grape vines.

On one occasion my brother Charles got stung on the forehead and had to stay home from work the next day. After that, I wanted to get stung so I could stay home.

There was plenty of work for people who were not afraid to get their hands dirty. Daddy was a hard worker, and no one could ever accuse him of being lazy. He would work from sunup to sundown; rise the next day to do it all over again.

Money grew on trees all right in California, but it was in the form of peaches, plums, oranges, and grapes, which belonged to the owner of the fields. I was so disillusioned that I wanted to give up at the ripe old age of five.

Daddy decided to take the family and go up the San Joaquin valley and work the fruit. It started with grapes somewhere outside Salinas, California. We slept in our car for a while, and then daddy bought a large tent, at least it seemed large to me. It was probably about 10 ft by 20 ft, but it was big enough for all of us to sleep in and we didn't have to sleep on the ground.

If we were going to make money, we had to learn how to cut grapes. When we got to the fields, we were given a grape knife, which looked very much like a linoleum knife that had a short handle with a curved blade. That made it easy to cut the stem on the cluster of grapes without losing the grapes. It was much easier than pulling them off the vine.

The grapes were cut and placed in a wooden crate about 18" by 24" and about 8" tall. The boxes would be filled and left in the field under the vines. When the vineyard was completely picked, we then would go back over it, and pour the grapes out onto a raisin board. We placed them in the middle of the row so the sun could shine on them and dry them out. I have often seen some of these old raisin boards in antique shops, with pictures painted on them.

Later, we would come back and place another board on top of the raisins and flip it over to allow the other side of the grapes to dry. After all the grapes were dried, we would bring a board with a paper covering the board and flip the grapes, which had now become raisins and we would let them dry a few days more. After they had all dried, we would come back again and roll the grapes up in the paper, and this was called cigarette rolling.

After the grapes were all dried and rolled, the final step in the process was to gather the rolls of raisins and pour them out in boxes for pickup. They would then be sent to the raisin plant for processing.

We often had to move from one place to another just to follow the work. There were grapes, peaches, plums, apricots, and many other varieties of fruit.

Later in the fall we picked cotton. Cotton grows on tall green stalks with a small, closed ball on the end. When it's ready to be picked, the cotton ball turns brown and opens to reveal the cotton inside. It was then time to head for the fields and spend your days pulling the cotton out of those hard brown cotton bowls and stuffing it in a long canvas bag that's pulled behind you in the row. By the end of the day your hands are cut and bleeding from the hard brown hulls and your back is hurting from pulling that sack all day.

Everyone had to pick when it was ready, even the little ones. Their sacks were shorter than the adults, but every little bit helped. When your sack was full, you would drag it to the weigh wagon where it would be weighed and dumped into the wagon. At the end of the day, you would go to the weigh wagon and draw your pay. If you were a good picker, you might have picked a hundred pounds in a day. At three cents a pound, you could make three dollars a day.

My Daddy could pick 200 lbs. of cotton a day and he could never understand why I could only pick 100 lbs. a day. He said I was younger and shorter than he and should be able to pick more than he could. No matter what, I was never a very good cotton picker. I made myself a promise that when I grew up, I would never pick cotton again. That's a promise I have kept to this day.

The San Joaquin valley would be just a giant desert if it were not for the California Aqueduct. As you drive through the Mojave Desert, and into the central valley of California, you wonder how this desert could become such a great fruit producing land. It's all because of the manmade river that flow over 400 miles to bring water to the valley.

The idea for the aqueduct started with an Irish immigrant named William Mulholand. Mulholand began buying up land to use in building a concrete ditch to bring water from the Colorado River to Southern California. The aqueduct begins near Parker Dam on the Colorado River and crosses the Mojave Desert, flowing around several small mountain ranges and around the San Jacinto Mountains west of Palm Springs and terminates at Lake Mathews in Riverside County.

The aqueduct was constructed between 1933 and 1941, mainly to bring water to the Los Angeles area. This project alone employed 30,000 people over an eight-year period. It was the largest public works project in California conducted during the Great Depression. In 1955, this project was recognized by the American Society of Civil Engineers as one of the "Seven Engineering Wonders of American Engineering".

When we arrived in California in 1941, the population of the Central Valley was about one million. Today, it is well over five million. Nearly five hundred miles long and about 50 miles wide, the Central Valley was a migrant workers' paradise. California has led the nation in total farm production every year since 1948. In its 50th consecutive year as the nation's top agricultural producer, the state exports over 12 billion dollars in agricultural production. It's interesting to note that nine of the nation's top ten counties in agriculture production are in California and six of these are in the Central valley.

After our first year of picking fruit all over the valley, we settled in a tent camp outside of Clovis, California called "Jimmie's Camp". It was a migrant camp like so many others throughout the valley. Everyone lived in tents with no running water or bathroom facilities. There was a community bathhouse in the center of the camp where you could take a shower. There were pipes of running water just outside each tent for the personal use of each family. With all the family working in the vineyards, we soon had enough money to build a wood floor in our tent.

I remember the day my Daddy brought the wood planks home to build the floor. We felt like we had arrived, because not everyone had a wooden floor in their tent. I thought we were special and were richer than most of the other people in the camp. We had plenty of food and money for an occasional coke or candy bar. Occasionally we could buy a taco, which costs a nickel. I felt I had a lot to be thankful for, and just being with my brother and sister was all I really wanted anyway.

On the other side of the road from Jimmy's Camp, was an old airfield that had been turned into a Japanese Concentration Camp. All the Japanese people who lived in the Fresno area were rounded up and brought to the camp. It didn't make any difference whether they were citizens. If they were of Japanese descent or even looked Japanese, they were brought to the camp and were held prisoner until the end of the war. This was called the Japanese American Internment Program and refers to the relocation of Japanese Americans living in the United States and more specifically those residing on the West Coast of the United States. More than 150,000 Japanese Americans were interned. Sometimes we would go over to the tall wire fence and talk to the boys and girls being held inside. I guess everybody thought that because they were Japanese, they might be traitors.

The Japanese people lived in big, long barracks, with only sheets hung between each family for privacy. They were put into these camps, not because they had been tried and found guilty of anything, but because, either they or their parents, or ancestors were from Japan. They were deemed a "threat" to national security. They were also easily identifiable, due to their race; however, there were no similar large-scale roundups of German or Italian-Americans, even though we were also fighting against them during WWII. Our government treated them as prisoners of war, and I guess we believed it was all right to put them in camps. After all, they were Japs', and they were our enemies. We now realize how wrong it was to take our own citizens and put them in concentration camps simply because of their race.

Aunt Oleta and Uncle Doyle came to visit us at Jimmy's Camp one day and asked if they could take Mary Ellen home with them. Beulah for some odd reason said no, she could not go. Now, Aunt Oleta had half raised Mary Ellen and she was not going to take no for an answer. She told Mary Ellen to go get her things; she was going home with her. Beulah stepped in Mary Ellen's way and said, "You are not going anywhere". Then she began to scream and curse at Aunt Oleta. She stepped over the line when she called Aunt Oleta a "Red Headed Peckerwood" (Aunt Oleta had red hair). That was too much for Aunt Oleta to take, so she plowed into Beulah. It took Daddy and Uncle Doyle both to pull them apart, all the while Beulah yelling at Daddy to let her go. It was a fight to behold, hair pulling, scratching, cursing. I don't know who won, but Mary Ellen went home with Aunt Oleta that night.

After we had been at Jimmy's Camp for about two years, daddy got a job with the labor union in Fresno. We continued to live in the tent city for a while, but soon Daddy rented a house on the outskirts of Clovis, and for the first time in a long while, we were living in a real house again. By this time the Hill family had increased to seven. Beulah had given birth to two girls, Donna Sue, and Bertha Marie. Not only was our family growing, but also the problem of taking care of all these kids were growing as well. Daddy's work took him out of town for weeks at a time and during that time we were left under the care of Beulah. She was only a young girl herself, and things began to change.

Soon there were problems between Beulah and Charlie, Mary Ellen, and me. Beulah began to complain to Daddy that it was too much for her to take care of all these children, and that he had to do something. Of course, I didn't know what was happening; only that Beulah had become more and more abusive. She often beat us with belts or other objects, whatever she could get her hands on.

One day after getting into trouble, she put me in a room and locked me in until my Daddy came home. She began to tell him about how bad I had been that day, and that I needed a good beating. When he arrived, I could hear them talking in the living room. She started to scream and demanded he beat me, so after a few minutes he came into my room taking off his big wide leather belt as he came. He closed the door behind him and came over to the bed where I sat. I had already filled my pants with cardboard, but to my surprise he said, "OK, I'm going to beat this pillow and you are going to yell." So, he began to beat that pillow and I began to yell. I know she must have thought he was killing me from the way I screamed and yelled. It was the best whipping I never got.

I know in fiction stepmothers are often looked at as being bad or wicked women, often portrayed like the stepmother in Cinderella, or Snow White. Most examples of their cruelty are stepdaughters or young girls, that become victims after the marriage. Although this scenario is not always accurate, this was the case with Daddy's new wife. When my sister, Mary Ellen, was about five years old, she was washing dishes, and dropped a dish and broke it. Beulah, our stepmother grabbed her and held her down while she poured a bottle of Louisiana hot sauce down her throat as punishment. I don't think Beulah had read many books on child development.

Unfortunately, Mary Ellen often got the worst treatment at the hands of our stepmother, I suppose, because she was too little to run, or defend herself. Things became so bad that the three of us decided to "kill" Beulah Mae. We set about planning our deed. Since Charles was the oldest it was decided he should be the one to strike the first blow. We hid our weapons around the living room and planned to attack her when she returned home from shopping.

Charles had a baseball bat behind the living room couch. I hid a butcher knife under the seat of the lounge chair. Mary Ellen was too small, but she wanted to help if she could. We talked about how much better off we would be once we killed Beulah. We tried to keep our courage up by talking, but soon we stopped talking and just waited. When the car drove up in the driveway we got up and waited for her to enter the door. As soon as she opened the door she started yelling and it scared us all and we ran out of the living room and hid. That was the end of our plan to get rid of our stepmother.

I have often thought about that day. What if we had gone through with our plot? Our lives would have been ruined and we would have all gone to jail or at least placed in juvenile custody for a very long time. I know God was looking out for me. Even before I knew Him, He had His hand on me.

Grandma, Grandpa, Charles, Mary and me, in Okmulgee

CHAPTER 7

Back to Oklahoma

I GUESS DADDY was feeling more pressure from Beulah, because one day he announced he was sending the three of us back to Oklahoma to live. He had called Uncle Doyle, who had gone back to his ranch in Oklahoma to live, and asked if he could send the three of us, back to live with him. Uncle Doyle and Aunt Oleta agreed and shortly thereafter we were on a Greyhound bus headed for Okemah, Oklahoma.

All three of us lived with Uncle Doyle for a couple of years. Living on the farm was some of the best times of our lives. Uncle Doyle bought us a horse and we had cows, chickens, and hogs. It was great living on the ranch. On Saturdays we would hitch up the team of horses to our wagon and go into the town of Okemah to sell our cream and eggs. Sometimes we would sell an animal or two.

One of the great things about going to town on Saturday was we always got to buy an ice cream cone. They cost five cents each, which was a lot of money, but we didn't think about the cost. We always looked forward to Saturdays. If Uncle Doyle was going to go to the auction, we sometimes were allowed to go to the movies. Now, that was a real treat! Saturday matinees with Roy Rogers or Gene Autry, it just didn't get any better than that. Saturday night was churning time. Aunt Oleta would give us all a large jar, half filled with cream, and we would start shaking it back and forth until it turned to butter, all the while listening to the Grand Old Opry on the battery radio. These batteries were the same type used in the car and we didn't have any extra, so on Saturday night, Uncle Doyle would take the battery out of the car and hook it up to the radio.

When the butter was all churned and the Grand Old Opera was over, we would all go to bed, and he would replace the battery in the car. Uncle Doyle worked hard on that old farm and Aunt Oleta worked right along beside him. We raised most of our own food and Aunt Oleta was good at sewing. If she had the right print she would make us a shirt, or Mary Ellen a dress from a flour sack that had been filled with cow feed . . . Uncle Doyle bought his cow feed in fifty-pound bags that had a print on the bag. After the bags were emptied of feed, Aunt Oleta would wash them and use them for cloth in her sewing.

One of the tragedies of working on that old ranch was, it made Uncle Doyle and Aunt Oleta old before their time. Work on the ranch was hard and they never seemed to stop. Often, Uncle Doyle would hire himself and his two horses "Pat and Blue" out to work for a neighbor. When the new road came through from Henrietta to Okemah, Uncle Doyle was hired to build the roadbed using his two horses and a skid. The work was hard, but the pay was good, and every little bit helped.

I remember a big winter storm coming through one year. Uncle Doyle put all three of us in a big feather bed and covered us with quilts so we would stay warm. When we woke up in the morning the room was covered with snow. It had blown in between the cracks in the wall during the night and covered everything with a powdery white film of snow.

Uncle Doyle made us stay in bed until he could go down to the pond and chop out a large chunk of ice. He built a fire outside the house and melted the ice so he could pour it into the radiator of his old car. After he got the car started, he put quilts in the rumble seat, carried us out, tucked us in and we headed for Okmulgee, to Grandma's house.

Mom and her new husband Philip Berch

CHAPTER 8
Mama's New Marriage

MAMA HAD REMARRIED and was living in Bakersfield, California with her new husband, Philip Berch. Phil was a painter and wallpaper contractor and made a good living. He had recently returned to California, after serving on an aircraft carrier in the pacific during WWII. Early in her marriage to Phil, Mama asked Daddy if she could have Mary Ellen and raise her in Bakersfield. Of course, Dad said yes, and Mary Ellen went to live with Mama in Bakersfield.

Mama had a daughter with her new husband who they named Connie Faye. Charles and I were still living with Uncle Doyle in Oklahoma, and I began to ask Daddy if I could come back to California and live with him. I had started to complain about the work on the ranch and I thought if I could get back to California, things would be different this time. He finally said I could, and I hitched a ride with one of Grandpa Petree's sons who was going to California to find work. This was one of the worst decisions I ever made, because things had not changed in the Hill household since I had been away.

Beulah was still abusive and unconcerned about my welfare, so most of the time I was left alone and had to fend for myself. When I was nine years old, I was living with my Daddy in Clovis, and I wanted to go visit my Mama who lived about 100 miles away in Bakersfield. Daddy was working off in the mountains and only came home on weekends, so I asked my stepmother if

I could hitchhike to Bakersfield to see my Mama and she said "sure". She didn't care what I did if I stayed out of her way.

So, I headed out for Bakersfield hoping my Mama would be glad to see me. Hitchhiking was my only way of transportation in those days, and it didn't seem to be as dangerous as it is now. I knew if the police saw me hitchhiking, they would pick me up, and take me back home, so I was very careful to look for the police while sticking out my thumb. I don't know how many times I hitchhiked to Bakersfield, but it was several times during that summer. A few times I would jump on a train when it slowed down, coming through Fresno and riding to Bakersfield, but that was dangerous and if the "Bulls" saw me, they would chase me out of the train yard. It was not easy jumping into the car of a moving train.

Mama had a job, working at a drive-in restaurant on old Highway 99, called "Budges Inn". US Highway 99 ran through the middle of Bakersfield, so all I had to do was get a ride to Bakersfield and walk to the restaurant.

Mama always seemed glad to see me, even though when I showed up it was always a surprise. She would always give me something to eat and drink and would usually buy me some new clothes before I went back home. There was a time when I got sick, she took me to the doctor and had my tonsils and adenoids removed. I was sick for a week. The great thing about having your tonsils taken out is you can have all the ice cream you wanted.

It was on one of those visits I learned to drink hot chocolate. It was a cold winter's day, a few days before Christmas and I walked into Budges Inn cold and hungry. Mama spotted me and asked if I wanted something to drink. I don't remember ever having hot chocolate before, but I had heard about it, so I said, "I'd take some of that." When she brought it over it was steaming hot with a big mound of whipping cream on top. As she walked away, I reached for a straw and stuck it in the hot chocolate. Before mama could stop me, I sucked on that straw and filled my mouth and throat with blazing fire. It was the first and last time I ever drank hot chocolate with a straw. As I spewed out the chocolate all over the counter, I yelled at the top of my lungs, and I thought I was going to die. Mama rushed over with a glass of ice water, but the damage was done. I have been a little afraid of hot chocolate ever since.

For the next several years Charles continued to live with Uncle Doyle and Aunt Oleta. I was always proud of Charles. He was the only one in our family at the time to ever graduate from high school. I think part of it may have been because of his participation on the high school baseball team. His team even won a state championship in his senior year. He loved sports and has passed that love down to his children and grandchildren.

He was the type of brother every little boy wants as his "big" brother. He was always looking after me and wouldn't let anyone pick on me. When Aunt Bonnie Ansiel's boy Sonny, took my bag of marbles, Charles beat him up and got back my marbles. On another occasion Beulah's brother pushed me around and tried to stop me from getting in Charlie's car. That was too much for my big brother, so Charlie dragged him out of the car, slapped him and told him to leave me alone. Even though he was bigger and older than me, he never bothered me again. I always felt safe when I was with Charlie. I lived with Daddy and Beulah in a house Daddy was renting in "Bean Town" just outside of Clovis, California. It was a small house, and I was given a bed on the back porch. It was all I needed because I wasn't home much. I could come and go as I pleased, day or night, no one seemed to care. Even though I was only about nine years old, I began to skip school and started running around with friends who were not a good influence on me. I couldn't seem to stay out of trouble; lying, cheating, stealing, and doing anything to cause problems. During this time, I began to smoke and drink and try to be like the older boys.

I joined a local gang and had to tattoo my initials on my arm (they are still there as a reminder of my initiation). My stepmother didn't seem to care what I did if I wasn't around the house. Often my clothes were so dirty and my jeans so stiff I could stand them up in the corner! For some odd reason I developed a love for reading and became an avid reader. I loved reading mostly Zane Gray books that my Daddy had laying around the house.

Daddy loved western books and he didn't care who read them after he got through with them. I always had one of those books with me wherever I went. Looking back, I realize it was the love of reading that helped me over the years. I didn't know it at the time, but because of a love for reading, I was able to discover the world in a way that I might never have known.

I was always looking for ways to make money whether it was legal or not. I learned early in my youth how to steal and cheat, often stealing from Daddy or Beulah. One man told me he would pay me a dollar to mow his lawn, so I got our old roller push mower out and mowed his lawn as best I could. It was a large lawn and the lawn mower I used was hard to push, it was before the invention of gasoline lawn mowers and had a round cylinder of blades that rotated. When I finally finished the job, I went to the house to get paid, and he said, "You didn't do a very good job so I'm not going to pay you" I cursed him out and left, dragging my mower behind me.

I wanted to get even with him so, that night I went back to his house and stole his water sprinkler. I don't know how he knew it was me that stole it, but the very next day, a policeman came to our house and told Daddy I had stolen Mr. Jones' water sprinkler. My Daddy assured him he would take care of it. After he left, Daddy called me and told me to bring him the sprinkler, which I did. He took me by the arm and drug me back to Mr. Jones's house, where he knocked on the door and made me give back the sprinkler also, I had to apologize. It was about the hardest thing I ever had to do. At that moment I hated my Daddy, Mr. Jones, the police, and most of the world.

School was not much fun for me. I was often sent to school hungry and without paper or pencil. I wasn't much for studying and didn't care about the grades I got, it just wasn't important.

I really can't remember how many grades I failed but again I didn't care, all I wanted was to turn sixteen and quit school.

Since I didn't have money for lunch, I was allowed to work in the cafeteria steam room for one hour every day during lunchtime. I scraped the trays and placed them in a rack and pushed them into the dishwasher. I was given lunch free and paid about a dollar a day, which was a lot of money for me, but after a while I messed that up somehow and was fired.

There came a time when I thought things were going to turn around for me. It was the summer of 1947 during the California State Fair which was held in Fresno. While walking around at the fair, I visited the cattle show and met the famous actor Victor McLaglen and his son Andrew who years later became a famous Hollywood director. I often see his name as director of old TV westerns such as Gunsmoke, and many others.

Victor McLaglen had a ranch outside Clovis, California and had brought his cattle to show them at the fair. He was seated on a bale of hay with some friends, drinking and having a good time. When he saw me, he called me over and asked me to run an errand for him. I spent the day and most of the night sitting there listening to his stories about his exploits as a prizefighter and an actor in England and Hollywood. For some reason he took a liking to me, so I told him my story of being on my own and trying to make my own way in life.

After a while he put his arm around me and asked if I would like to come to his ranch and live with him. I jumped at the thought of living on his ranch, and having somewhere to belong, and maybe even a chance to become the adopted son of Victor McLaglen. He told me he lived on a ranch up in the foothills just a few miles from Clovis. He even gave me directions on how to get to his house. He told me he wanted me to come and live with him on his ranch. He said, "We'll have a great time". Wow! My head was spinning, and I could hardly sleep at all that night waiting for the sun to come up, so I could start a new chapter in my life.

The next day I rode my bicycle from Clovis to his ranch which was about twenty-five miles up in the foothills, dreaming about my new life, all the way. When I finally got to his ranch, I rode my bicycle down a long winding road to his house while my heart was pounding with anticipation. His house was the biggest house I had ever seen. I could just see me living in one of those big rooms with servants and toys and anything I wanted to eat.

Mr. McLaglen was in a huge barn off to the side of his house and I could see him inside working on a horse collar. When I went into the barn and said hello, he hardly spoke. He asked me what I wanted, and I told him about our conversation the day before at the State Fair. He laughed and said, "I don't remember anything about yesterday, I was too drunk". He told me to run along home and forget I had ever met him. I couldn't believe what I was hearing. My heart was broken, and my dreams dashed again. The great actor, Victor McLaglen didn't even remember me.

Rio and Fay Rice

CHAPTER 9
Given Away

I DON'T REMEMBER much about that faithful day in the summer of 1947. Only that it was the worst day in my young life. Coming home from school, I noticed that all my belongings were in a cardboard box and sitting on the front porch. My stepmother came out of the house just as I got to the porch, and I asked her why all my stuff was outside. I'm sure she was happy as she said, "Your Daddy has given you away".

I sat on the porch wondering in my mind just what being given away meant. I didn't know what to think at the time. Surely it didn't mean given away forever. But, before long an old Dodge flatbed truck with sideboards about three feet high and a tarpaulin nailed over the top, pulled up in our yard. A tall slender man about forty years old got out. He grabbed my box from the front porch and threw it on that old truck. He turned and picked me up and tossed me in the back of that truck, along with everything else he was hauling under that tarp.

As we pulled away from my house, I could see my stepmother standing on the front porch with her broom, waving goodbye. I didn't know what was happening, but I had a sick feeling in my stomach as though something bad was happening.

What I didn't know at the time was that this man was taking me to Oklahoma, to work on his farm and that I would not see or hear from my Mama or Daddy or any of my family for several years. I was suddenly the property of a man I had never met and was taken far away from those I loved. I was sent to work as a farm hand, fifteen hundred miles away. It might as well have been a million miles away for that matter. I didn't think my life could get much worse than this, but I didn't know how hard farm work was. It was about to get worse, much—worse.

Nighttime was the worst time of all, not knowing what was going to happen to me. Crazy thoughts would fill my head. If I didn't work hard, would they give me to someone else? Would they beat me or even worse, would they kill me? When you are nine years old you don't know what to think. For many nights fear would grip my heart and I began to cry. I had gone through tough times before, but nothing compared with this. It all seemed like a bad dream, but it was real.

I hoped I would be here for only a few weeks and then they would send me back home. But that was not going to happen. When this strange man picked me up, I wasn't even given a chance to ask questions or to say goodbye to anyone. My Daddy was off working in the mountains, my brother was living with my uncle in Oklahoma and my sister was living with my Mama in Bakersfield, so in reality there was no one to share good-byes with.

Returning to Oklahoma was one of the saddest times in my life. For the first time in my life, I really felt alone. No family or friends to call my own. I felt isolated and worthless, like a piece of property with no rights of my own. I knew Lincoln had freed the slaves, but I felt somehow, he had neglected me.

The man, to whom I was given, Rio Rice and his wife, Faye had leased a 200-acre farm about 40 miles south of Tulsa, Oklahoma with the purpose of becoming farmers. The farm itself had a four-room wooden house with a large barn for the cattle and a small pond to water the stock. The bottom land along the creek was used to grow corn and several acres were set aside for cattle grazing while the rest was farmland.

It was Rio's intention to raise milk cows and grow cotton. Since he and Faye had only girls, I guess he thought a boy would come in handy working on the farm. He had made some sort of deal with my Daddy for me, and I never did find out what this deal was. What I did find out was that I belonged to him, lock, stock, and barrel and what he said was law.

Looking back, now that I have three children of my own, Holli, Doyle, and Chuck, I would without question die before I would let anyone take any one of them from me. I can't imagine the thought of being without them. I will never understand how my Daddy could give me away to anyone. For years I blamed myself for being a bad kid that no one wanted. I know there is some truth to that, but would that justify giving me away? Was I really that bad?

It's been difficult through the years to listen to sermons on fatherhood. When the reference is made to our Heavenly Father, and how He loves us like our own earthly father. I sometimes question that reasoning, if God is like our earthly father, I'm not sure I want to be His child.

The good news is I've learned God is not like our earthly father. He loves us when we are good, and He loves us when we are bad. He might have to chastise us occasionally, but he will never give us away.

My first two years with Rio in Oklahoma, I attended a one-room schoolhouse. It was within walking distance of our farm. There was no school bus anyway, so we all walked to school. It was a typical one-room schoolhouse with eight rows of seats. Each row was a different grade level. We had no plumbing or running water, and everyone had chores to do to get the day started.

Some of us had to clean the outhouse and make sure that it was well stocked. Others had to draw fresh water from the well and bring it in for drinking. Some of us had to clean the blackboards or sweep out the room. Men of the community would bring firewood to school for the big stove in the middle of the room. It was really a fun place to study the three "Rs", reading, riting, and rithmatic.

No one wore shoes unless it was very cold or snowing, and even then, we hated to wear them. Our teacher was quick to discipline us when we did something wrong and she was always supported by the parents, who were disgraced if their children misbehaved.

The instruments for discipline were hickory switches and dunce caps. There were times when a quick slap on the hand with a ruler would do the trick. The worst was to stand on our tiptoes with our nose in a circle drawn on the blackboard.

We didn't have a lunchroom, so we ate our lunch in the yard under a tree or sitting on the steps. We would wash our lunches with water from a well and if we had time we would run and play until the teacher rang her little bell.

There was a washbasin in the back of the classroom, and everyone shared it. Soap and towels were placed on a bench near the cloakroom at the entrance to the school. We washed up there for lunch and after playing in the dirt of the schoolyard at recess.

Nearly two years later we started going to school in the town of Beggs which was a few miles from our farm. A school bus would pick us up in front of our farmhouse and bring us back each afternoon. This school was bigger than our little one room school we had been attending. It had a different room for every grade and a teacher for each room. It even had a gymnasium where I learned to play basketball.

Farming is hard work and I soon learned that living on a farm meant working from sunup to sundown. At first, we had to plow the fields and prepare them for planting. Rio had an old Ford tractor with double turning plows; it was my job to plow the fields. During the spring I would plow from early morning until it was time to catch the school bus. I would plow until I saw the bus coming, then turn the tractor off and run to the house, grab a syrup bucket which contained my lunch, and head for the road to catch the bus. After school I would go back to the tractor where I had left it and continue to plow the field until dark.

Often in the summer, after I had finished my work on our farm, Rio would hire me out to other farmers to work for them. I could plow fields or bale hay or chop cotton and just about anything a man could do. There was always work to be done. We grew our own hay and would have to bale it and load it on the old truck and bring it to the barn. After that, we would stack it up in the loft for winter feed.

I stayed dirty most of the time, often washing my hands and face and putting on one of my two sets of clothes. I had one set of old clothes for working, and another for going to school. Faye would wash clothes every Monday, and iron every Tuesday. We would build a fire outside of the house and use a large black pot to heat the water. It was my job to keep the fire going and the pot full of water. Faye washed outside in a large galvanize washing tub, with a scrub board and lye soap. She would rinse them in another galvanized tub of clean water and then hang them on a clothesline Reo had constructed in the backyard. I don't know when washing machines were invented but whenever they were, we didn't have one.

I was also responsible for helping to milk the cows every morning and every evening. We had sixteen milking cows and they had to be milked by hand. I milked eight cows and Faye would milk the other eight. We would take the milk to the porch and separate the milk from the cream. After separating it we would then pour the cream into large milk cans and take them to the edge of the road so they could be picked up by the milk truck and taken to the dairy.

One of our old cows was a leader of the herd, and all the other cows would follow her to the barn. It was my job to go get them every evening from the bottomland for milking, and then we left them in the pen overnight so we could milk them again in the morning.

That old lead cow had a chain around her neck, and we all called her "Chainey". I used to ride her in from the bottomland, and always got into trouble when I got caught. I tried to remember to get off her just at the bottom of the last little hill leading to the barn, so I would not be seen and get in trouble. Rio was not a harsh or violent man, and never beat me. My punishment was always more work. There was plenty of that to go around.

In the spring we would plant cotton, soybeans, and corn for the market. We would also have a large garden for vegetables. One spring Rio heard about a new crop that would make lots of money, called castor beans. It was the bean that produced Castor Oil. It grew to be seven or eight feet tall, and the bean was inside a shell much like a cocklebur, with sharp barbs all over it. You could only pick it with thick gloves. It was by far the most difficult crop we ever planted.

I don't know why, but we only grew it that one year. Maybe he didn't make as much money as he had expected. I was glad we didn't grow it anymore because it was hard work picking those beans from their tall stalks. Cotton was our standard money crop, and Rio always grew as many acres of cotton as he was allowed.

The government would only allow us to grow a certain number of acres. It was called an allotment and we could either grow our allotment or we could sell it to someone else. Each crop started with plowing, then cultivating, planting, fertilizing, spraying for boll weevils, weeding, and hoeing to thin it out. Then the good time came of laying-by, a time of waiting for the harvest in the fall.

After the cotton was planted, it would be several weeks before it would come up, so this gave us time to swim and hunt, and do other things on the farm that needed attention. Fixing the fences, painting the barn, or white washing the trees were some of those things.

When the cotton came up and began to grow, we would have to thin the stalks, chop the grass and weeds. Chopping cotton was hard work and everybody got into the act. While we chopped, Rio would wait at the end of the rows with a large file and keep our hoes sharp. It was during this time I learned a good lesson. If anything is worth doing, it's worth doing right. In addition to me, Rio's girls, his nephews, and anyone who could handle a hoe, were hard at work chopping the grass out before it choked out the cotton stalks. As we chopped row after row, suddenly I came upon a lot of Johnson grass in my row. Everyone else was laughing and talking and went on with their way chopping and thinning. I was left far behind chopping my Johnson grass. Johnson grass is the hardest, meanest, toughest grass God ever allowed to grow on this earth. Why I was the one blessed with so much of it in my row I will never know. With everyone leaving me behind I decided to just top it and hurry on, half chopping and thinning so I could catch the other kids.

Late in the afternoon when we finished chopping for the day, we all headed for the swimming hole to go swimming. We all laid down our hoes and headed for the pond. Just as I was about to head for the pond, Rio called me over. He handed me another hoe and took me to the row I had half done and said, "After you do this row over the right way you can go swimming". Everyone headed for the pond, and I headed for the field. That was the last time I half did my work.

Although the work was hard and the hours long, I was not mistreated or abused, just worked hard. I never thought that Faye liked me much; I think it was because I was a boy and she had only girls. I would go with Rio to the auction or to town for supplies and the girls had to stay home. Faye thought Rio was spending too much time with me, and not enough time with his girls. She often let me know how she felt by saying things to hurt me.

Saturday night was bath night. Since we didn't have indoor plumbing, we would carry water in from the pump, and pour it into a galvanized wash tub, put some on the old wood burning stove to heat, and then pour that into the tub. Then everyone would take a bath. Faye first, then Rio, then the girls one after the other until all had taken a bath. I was always the last and by the time I took my bath there would be an inch of mud on the bottom of the tub. One of Grandma's sayings used to be, "you may be poor, but you don't have to be dirty." I don't know how clean I got being the last to take a bath on those Saturday nights, but it was the best we could do at the time.

On some Sundays we would get up early, do our chores and then get dressed for church, which simply meant putting on my one pair of good jeans and my good shirt. Occasionally we attended an old rock church near the town of Sapulpa, Oklahoma. I'm not sure what denomination it was, but the adults washed each other's feet every Sunday.

After the sermon there would be music playing and the kids played games while the ladies prepared the dinner on the ground. It was always a feast with fried chicken, mashed potatoes, pork salad, beans, and corn. There would always be desserts of apple pie, cake and if we could get the ice, we would churn homemade ice cream.

Sundays were always good, and I looked forward to the change. The only work we had to do was feed the animals and milk the cows. It seemed that everyone in that little church played a musical instrument of one type or another. All of Rio's brothers played stringed instruments, such as banjos, mandolins, guitars, fiddles, or bass. They even tried to teach me to play, but I didn't have the ear for it, and I soon sold my guitar.

Even though I missed my family, summers were the best of times. Hunting, fishing, and trapping was a young boy's dream. I always had a gun of some type, at first just a BB gun, then a 4-10 shotgun, and later a 22 rifle. I often wonder what happened to all my guns after I ran away from the farm.

One year Rio allowed me to build a small chicken house to raise fryers so I could sell them in the spring. I worked all winter on that chicken house, putting in feeders and a long electric cord to hang in the middle of the chicken house with a light bulb so it would keep the biddies warm. I ordered my chicks through the "Grit" newspaper, and they were sent through the mail. It was a great day when the mailman delivered my 100 newborn chicks. I built a feeding trough and had lids that screwed on fruit jars which would let out just enough water. All through the winter I fed, watered, and sprayed them for mites. I cleaned out the coops and closed them up at night so the foxes couldn't get to them. I was so proud of my chickens; I just knew I would make lots of money. During this time, they were getting big enough to sell and I was making plans on what I was going to do with my money.

One afternoon coming home from school on the bus, I could see smoke coming from behind the house. As I jumped off the bus and started to run home, tears began to fall down my face as I saw the little chicken house where all my chickens were on fire. What an awful sight. All my young chickens burned to a crisp. I couldn't hold back the hurt and started crying like a baby.

We never found out what happened. I always thought Faye started the fire, but I know she didn't. It was probably the electric wire I had run from the house to the chicken coop to keep them warm. Regardless of the cause, losing that little chicken house was one of my biggest disappointments.

I never had much money while living with the Rice's, but I never went hungry, cold or in real need of anything. It was a time of learning and time of growing up. I learned to be independent, to make good decisions (most of the time) and take charge of my life.

My first date ever, was to a school dance. It was when I was in the fifth grade, and I had a girlfriend. Since I couldn't drive a car, I asked Rio if I could pick her up on the farm tractor. Rio consented and even helped me build a seat out of wood between the fender and the tractor seat. Her farm was just down the road from ours and so I picked her up and drove her to the school dance. We had a great time and I guess that was my only time driving a convertible to school.

When I was about thirteen, I decided to run away from the farm. I visited my grandmother in Okmulgee and while there I talked to my cousin Sammy Ansiel. We decided to run away and go to California. One day after school instead of coming home, I hitched a ride to Okmulgee and hooked up with Sammy. We started hitchhiking and got as far as Oklahoma City, where we were caught and brought back. They watched me a little more closely after that.

I went back to the little school in the town of Beggs, Oklahoma, and when I was in the sixth grade, I made the basketball team. We only had about a dozen boys in the sixth grade, so it wasn't hard to make the team. We had uniforms and played at other schools, and it was a great time for me.

Since we didn't have a lunchroom, we had to bring our lunch from home. My lunch usually consisted of two biscuits, one filled with whatever we had left over from the night before, a slice of ham or maybe a piece of bacon or chicken, and the other one with some jam or honey in it. I don't ever remember eating beef on the farm. Beef was a cash crop, only to be sold for money. If a calf was born and it was a heifer, it would become a milk cow, if it was a bull, it would become a steer, fattened up and sold. We never killed a beef cow to eat. So, my lunches consisted of whatever we had left from breakfast or the night before. The other biscuit would be filled with jelly or something sweet.

I guess you could consider us poor, but so were most of our friends, and we didn't think about being poor, we were just kids living on a farm. I do remember the first time I ever saw potato chips. One day during lunchtime, we all took out our sacks and buckets and sat in a circle to eat and talk. One boy who we considered rich (his dad owned a store in town) opened his sack lunch and took out a small bag of potato chips. I wondered to myself, "what will they think of next"? He shared his chips with the group, and they were about the best thing I had ever tasted.

We were never able to buy soda pop or candy. It was too much of a luxury and we always had to share when we were ever lucky enough to get any of those things. I can still remember thinking, "when I grow up, I'm going to buy me a soda pop and a candy bar and eat it and drink it all by myself, without having to share it with anyone." I also made myself a promise, that when I grew up, I would never be broke. I would always have money in my pocket. That's a promise I have always tried to keep. I have a little hideaway in my wallet, and I always have a few dollars hidden away in the pocket of that wallet. Uncle Doyle had a saying, "I'm not broke, just badly bent". I know now what he was talking about.

I learned a lot during the time I spent with the Rio Rice family on that little farm between Beggs and Sapulpa, Oklahoma. I learned how to hunt and trap animals and was allowed to keep the money I got from selling the furs to buy school clothes. There was a small creek that ran through the bottomland of our farm, and it was teaming with all kinds of wild critters. During the winter, I always had traps set. I would catch raccoons, muskrat, opossum and occasionally even a mink. I would skin them and nail them to a drying board, shaped much like an ironing board, only smaller. After the hides dried, I would bundle them up and take them into town to sell. I always had more opossum than I did anything else. I guess they were more plentiful, or maybe just dumber than the other animals. The opossum would sell for twenty-five cents, while the raccoon would bring fifty cents and the mink, and the fox would bring a dollar or two.

We always kept hunting dogs and it was said that Rio had a dog, that all he had to do was put his drying board out by the back steps and his dog would go out and get an opossum, or coon to fit the board. Everything was fine until one day Faye put her ironing board out by the back steps and that poor dog took off and hasn't been seen since.

Coon hunting was always fun in Oklahoma. We would get our carbide light hat, rifles, call the dogs and away we would go. The dogs always ran ahead of us. You could tell by the barking whether or not they were on a trail, because when they treed a coon, they would change their bark to a howl, and we knew they had him up a tree.

When we would get to the tree where the dogs were, they would be jumping and barking trying to climb that tree and get that coon. The old coon would be up on a limb and be growling like he wanted those dogs to just try and come get him. We would shine our lights up into the tree until we found whatever it was the dogs had treed. We would try to shoot the animal out of the tree without shooting him in the body. Shooting an animal in the head in the dark was no easy job. If we shot a hole in the body, the skin would not bring as much as a clean head shot. I got pretty good at shooting a 22 rifle and could usually shoot a coon through the head in the middle of the night with only my carbide light to see him. This came in handy in later years when I joined the Air Force. I received the Sharp Shooters Metal in basic training and was the best shot in our company.

One special Saturday night Rio said he had a treat for us. We were all going down the road to our neighbor's farm and watching the Lone Ranger on television. We never had a television, but our neighbor had one, and on Saturday night he would bring it out on his porch and all the neighbors would come and sit on his porch and watch TV. The two shows I remember were "The Lone Ranger", and "The Cisco Kid".

Usually, we would have some cookies and milk or even lemonade occasionally. The television was about nine inches round in a cabinet about the size of a chest of drawers. Often there was so much "snow" on the screen you could hardly see the actors. Watching TV and the change of pace from our regular, hard workweek made Saturday night the best night of the week.

There were many times during those years I was so lonely and homesick to see my family I would just lie down in the grass and have a good cry. I remember one spring day as I was on my way to the bottomland to get the cows. I lay down on the tall grass and cried for what seemed like hours. It was cold enough for a coat and the wind was blowing, so lying down in the tall grass kept the wind from coming through that thin coat. I could feel the sun as it shined down on that little spot. As I lay there in the grass feeling sorry for myself, I began to cry out to God. "Doesn't anyone love me?" What I didn't know at that time was, there was someone who loved me, but it would be many years before I found out whom that someone was. I soon decided to run away again.

Grandma, Aunt Edith, James and me

CHAPTER 10
Living with Grandma

THE LAST TIME I ran away from the farm, I decided to take nothing with me except the little money I had saved up from selling coon and opossum skins, and working for Mr. Bridges on the farm next to ours.

My plan was to go to California, but I didn't know how it was going to happen. What I did know was that I had to get away from that farm. One morning after I got off the bus at school, I walked to the highway and began hitchhiking. I got a ride as far as Okmulgee and decided to go to my Grandma's house and see if I could stay with her. Grandma let me stay with her, and when Rio and his brothers came looking for me, I hid in her bedroom. Grandma went out in the yard to talk to Rio, and I don't know what she told him, but he soon went away. Rio never came to look for me again, and I never knew why. I don't know what Grandma said to him that day he came looking, but whatever it was, I never went back to the farm again. I learned some years later that Rio and Faye had gotten a divorce. I always wondered if it had anything to do with me.

School was almost out for the summer, so I didn't enroll in school and Grandma said I had to get a job. Being only fourteen I didn't know what kind of job I could get. One day Grandpa Petree came home from work and said he had gotten me a job at the milk company.

In those days, milk was delivered every morning to the customer's door. The milk company provided a metal box with four compartments that held one quart each, to be left by the door for the deliveryman to refill.

If you wanted one quart, you just put out one empty bottle, if you wanted more you put out as many quarts as you wanted. You could also get orange juice, chocolate milk, buttermilk and even punch, if you left a note.

Grandpa said he had gotten me a job delivering milk with our milkman. So, the milkman would come around in his milk truck every day at four o'clock in the morning and pick me up. We would go to the dairy and load up all the cases of milk and other items for the day's delivery. It was part of my job to run to each house on the street that had a milk box out by the door, then take it back to the truck and fill the order.

I worked six days a week, usually from four to nine A.M. After we made all the deliveries we had to go back to the plant and unload all the empty bottles, clean out the truck and get ready for the next day's run.

The pay wasn't great, but the work was steady. I could even work during the winter up until about eight o'clock and the milkman would drive by the school and let me off. During school days I didn't have to unload the truck, but there was always something that had to be done at the milk factory.

Grandma never charged me anything for staying at her house. She let me have all the money I made for clothes and other things I needed. I was able to save up a little money that I used later for my return to California.

Charles, Mary, and me

CHAPTER 11

On the Road Again

I LIVED WITH Grandma about a year before I decided to return to California. Grandpa Petree had a son named Gene who was seventeen years old and had a car. It wasn't much of a car, but it would run. It was a twelve-cylinder Packard and used gas like it was going out of style, but back then gas was only 25 cents a gallon. Gene asked me if I wanted to go to California with him, and by that time I was ready to go. I packed my belongings, said good-bye to Grandma, and at the ripe old age of fifteen I headed back to California.

I don't know how much money we had, but it wasn't much. We traveled during the day, and at night we would pull over and sleep in the car. We arrived in California late in the fall, when most of the fruit had already been harvested, but we were able to pick up a few jobs as we headed north.

We picked cherries around Sacramento, and then we heard there was work in Oregon in the lumber mills, so we moved on. We were able to get jobs in a lumber mill near Eugene, Oregon and started to work on Monday of the next week. With no money and no place to stay, we started looking for somewhere to live. We found an old, abandoned shack deep in the woods not too far from the mill. It was a one-room building with an old barrel in the middle that was used as a stove. We made ourselves beds in the one room and tried to cover the windows to keep the cold out. There was plenty of wood around that old shack, so we built a fire and went to sleep.

The next day we went looking for food. We were broke and hungry and didn't know what we were going to do. We walked around the town and saw a house with several rabbit hutches out behind the house. That night we went back to the house and stole a couple of their rabbits. We left the hutch door open so the people would think the rabbits got out during the night. We had also noticed a garden in the back of one of the houses in town and that night we went by and picked some of their vegetables. We cooked the rabbit and vegetables together in an old pot we found in the shack and had rabbit stew. Those rabbits fed us for several days.

We also learned that the large grocery stores got delivery of bread and bananas early in the morning before the store opened. They just stacked them up by the backdoor. Over the next couple of weeks, we ate bread and bananas and anything else that was left. I guess you could say we learned to do our shopping early before the stores opened!

When we started working at the lumber mill, I was given the job of taking off the rough slabs after the first cut. It was called the "Green Line" because it was green lumber. That was some of the hardest work I had ever done, and it made me wonder why I ever left the farm in Oklahoma. At least I had a warm bed, and good food, even if the work was hard.

Gene and I worked every day for two weeks and then on Friday we went to get our pay. The owner told us he couldn't pay us, because we didn't have social security cards and we were underage.

We were told to get off the property and not to come back; as if we would. We decided to go back to California again and try to find work. We loaded up our few belongings and headed for Sacramento. The problem was we still didn't have any money, so we were up that preverbal creek without a paddle again.

As always, we had a five-gallon can and a short piece of water hose (Oklahoma Credit Card). When we needed gas, we would just wait until night, then find a car or truck out of the way of people or near a house so we could not be seen.

When everyone was asleep and no one was around, one of us would act as lookout while the other slipped up to the car and siphoned out the gas. After taking off the gas cap, we had to insert the hose in the tank and suck on the end of the hose until the gas started coming out. At this point we had to act quickly so we wouldn't fill our mouth with gasoline. We would put the other end of the hose in the gas can and wait until the can was full, pull out our hose and head back to our car. We did that every night coming from Washington to California.

Once we blew a tire on that old Packard and we didn't have a spare. We walked into the nearest town and started looking for a pickup truck that had the same size tire mounted on the outside of the truck with the same hole pattern as the wheel on our car. After walking around for several hours, we finally found the right truck. That night we took a lug wrench to the house where we had located the pickup and quietly removed the spare from the truck. We took the tire back to our car; we always kept a sharp eye out for the police that might be patrolling. As soon as it was fixed, we were on our way again.

After several days we ran out of money again and didn't have anything to eat so we decided to break into a grocery store. We cased a small "mom and pop" type grocery store and decided that we would break in that night and steal something to eat. As darkness fell, we both were having second thoughts, but the hunger pains overtook our fright and we decided to go ahead with our plan. Around midnight we went around to the back of the store and broke the lock with the tire iron. We quietly made our way in and began to search for things to steal.

Food, money, cigarettes, anything we thought we could use. We didn't find any money, but we took everything else we could carry. I have often thought about that low point in my life and wondered if there was any way I could repay the people who owned that little store. I decided that there are some things you can't go back and change, some things you just leave with God. He forgives and part of your repentance is remembering the things you did and can't undo.

Somewhere along the way, near Sacramento we saw a sign that said, "Cherry Pickers Wanted". We stopped a few days and picked cherries. We would sleep in the car and use the public restroom for washing up. Cherry picking wasn't a great job, but we were glad to get work and we stayed until the picking ran out, then it was time to move on. When we arrived back in California, Gene decided to go to his brother and see if he could stay with him, so we parted company after being together for several months. It was several years before I saw Gene again. He later became a police officer somewhere in Arkansas, and I wonder if he ever thought about that store we broke into, or of our other petty thievery?

I wandered around for a few months, working where I could. I got a job making peach packing boxes. Sometimes worked in the fields doing whatever I could to earn money. I picked cotton, cut grapes, picked, and packed peaches, picked plums, dried grapes for raisins, caprified, (cross pollinate) and picked figs. There was work in the fields almost year-round in California, and though it was low paying, you could earn enough to live.

One day after returning to Clovis, California I was wandering around town when suddenly out of nowhere, I turned the corner and ran into my Daddy. I mean I literally ran into him. He took a step back and said, "Well Peewee, how are you doing?" I said, "I'm doing fine" We exchanged small talk for a few minutes and then he said, "well I have to go, take care of yourself", and he went on his way. I was fifteen or sixteen at the time and had not seen him for several years, but it was as though we were just old friends and hadn't seen each other for a while.

At the time it didn't seem a big deal, but in later years I wondered how he could just walk away like that. I know my Daddy loved me, but he had a hard time showing it. I can't ever remember him telling me he loved me. It was just something he didn't do. My Daddy was a hard worker, a man without any education, and everything he knew he learned the hard way, through the school of hard knocks.

Daddy loved hard liquor, but he could not handle it, and often got drunk. I suppose, this was to forget his troubles. There were many times when he would come home drunk and have a big fight with Beulah, his wife. On one occasion they got into a big fight over something he said or did. He was drunk, and she was mad, and the fight began. After fighting for a while, she went into the kitchen and got a butcher knife and came out threatening to kill him. He tried to take the knife away and she stabbed him in the back of the neck, blood went everywhere. I thought she had killed him. She tied it up and somehow got him into the car and took him to the hospital where they sewed it up and sent him back home. The term "domestic abuse" had not yet made its way into the American vocabulary, so life went on as usual.

There was always trouble in our house and fighting was a way of life. On one occasion Daddy brought his girlfriend home to iron a shirt for him and for some reason Beulah got mad. Can you imagine that? I felt sorry for the poor girl. I don't think she knew Daddy was married.

Daddy would give you the shirt off his back if you asked, but he would steal it back the next day if he had the opportunity. He taught us that stealing wasn't wrong, it was only wrong if you got caught.

I had dropped out of school when I left Grandma's and had been bumming around Clovis for about a year. I sometimes stayed with a friend, or often would just sleep wherever I could. I made a little sleeping area with cardboard boxes on the north end of the old Clovis High School, between the building and the hedge. It wasn't the best situation, but it worked for a while.

I am convinced one of the most important parts of a person's life is education. Not everyone is able to go to college, but almost everyone is able to get a high school diploma. I am convinced the more education you have the greater possibility of success you have.

My home away from home became the "Clovis Pool Hall" owned by a Mexican man who let me work, doing odd jobs, cleaning up and racking balls in the poolroom. I became a pretty good pool player and could win enough money during the week to pay for the things I needed. I also helped as a short order cook, fixing Tacos at the grill. I guess that's where I learned to love Mexican food. I would clean up the public restrooms in Clovis Park and eat at one of the many restaurants in Clovis.

I began running with a bad crowd, drinking, and getting into trouble. Although I never went to jail, I was known on a first name basis with the local police officers. There was a time when three or four of us were drinking "sneaky peek" wine, (cheap white wine and lemon juice) when we were stopped by the Clovis police. None of us were of the age to drink. So, we thought we were in big trouble. Instead of taking us to jail, they took us all out to a swimming hole where we often hung out, and threw us in, clothes and all.

As I look back on it now, I often wonder what would have happened to me had I not gone into the U.S. Air Force. Several years after I married and was living in Florida, I returned to the little town of Clovis, California and wandered around trying to remember people and incidents from my past.

I remembered the Recardi brothers whom I ran around with and who were my best friends. I visited the bar on the corner of Clovis Ave., where we hung out. Even though I was only a teenager at the time, I idolized the Recardi brothers and wanted to be like them. They were cool guys and we had lots of fun together.

I asked around as to where they were and was told that Johnny had gotten into a fight a few years back and died on the sidewalk outside that same bar, strangled on his own blood. Jimmy was in prison serving life for killing a man. But, for the grace of God, that could have been me.

Me in the Air Force

CHAPTER 12

Air Force

ON SEPTEMBER 3, 1955 I made one of the most important decisions of my life. I decided I would enlist in the United States Air Force. Being only seventeen at the time I had to have my parent's signature to agree for me to enlist. This was a problem for me, because I hadn't lived at home in some time and I didn't know if my Daddy would sign or not, and even if he would I was not sure I wanted to ask him. It had been a long time since I had asked my Daddy for anything, and I wasn't comfortable asking him for this. I finally decided if I was going to enlist, I had to have his signature, so I took the form and went to his house.

When I knocked on his door, he was there, and came outside to talk. I asked him if he would sign for me to go into the Air Force, he said he was glad to, and on September the 16, 1955 I enlisted for four years in the United States Air Force.

I enlisted in Fresno, California, but the real induction took place in San Francisco, where I was sent to Parks Air Force Base for basic training. Basic training was hard for me because I was not used to taking orders. I was punished several times for my rebellious spirit. I kept thinking it would take me only a few months for these people to come around to my way of thinking. It took six months for me to realize it would be much better for me if I came around to their way of thinking.

I didn't like basic training very much. Up at 4:00 A.M. to clean the barracks, shower, shave (what little fuzz there was) and get dressed in fatigues for the day. Chow was served at 6:00 A.M., school started at 7:00 A.M., which lasted until 11 A.M. School was not a school where we learned to read and write. It was a school to teach us the ins and outs of military life. We learned to disassemble our weapons, then clean and reassemble them. We learned military protocol, the Air Force handbook, and the proper way of dressing. After we had lunch, we would spend the afternoon in military training (marching). I will always be grateful for the training I had in the Air Force.

For the first time in my life, I felt like I had something to belong to, a family that I cared for, and a family that cared for me. I had a roof over my head (most of the time), food to eat and clothes that were clean, starched and ironed. I also had a bed to sleep in and a paycheck every month. The pay wasn't that great, $64.00 a month, but it was more than I ever had before, and I couldn't complain.

After three months of training, we received a 24-hour pass. We boarded the busses and headed for San Francisco. Why the Air Force turned young raw recruits loose on San Francisco I will never know. What I do know is, we soon broke down and headed back to the base. We may not have been ready for San Francisco, but San Francisco was ready for us!

After Basic Training I was ready to serve our country. In February of 1956, I graduated from Basic Training and received my first stripe, what a thrill it was sewing it on, Airman Third Class Olan Hill. Mary Lou, my wife, has always said I was never "Third Class", but she and the Air Force had a difference of opinion.

Sometime during our basic training, we were given a questionnaire to fill out. One of the questions we were asked was "can you type?" Since I had taken a course in typing in high school I replied, "yes" to that question. When I received my orders, I was assigned duty as a company clerk typist. I didn't realize it at the time, but it turned out to be a great assignment.

I had mentioned to my drill instructor that I wanted to be a pilot, so one day he said to follow him. He gave me my new assignment "pick this trash up here and pile it over there". His idea of "Pilot" and mine were a little different.

I was given two weeks leave of absence and told to report to Fairchild AFB in Spokane, Washington, where I was assigned to the 2nd Bombardment Wing. The base was part of the Strategic Air Command (SAC) and was home of the B-36 Peacemaker.

The weather in Spokane for the most part is cold and wet. It rained or snowed almost daily during the winter months. Even in the summer it's cold and rainy almost every day. The joke of Fairchild AFB was that you would be taken up in a B-36 once a month, so you could see the sunshine.

For the majority of my time in the service, I was inside with very little manual labor. My duties were mostly nine to five with evenings off, which gave me time to go to night school and pursue a High School Diploma.

My commanding officer called me into his office one day and said he had been going over my records and noticed that I had not finished high school. He told me about a program called the GED, where I could finish my high school work and get a high school equivalence diploma. I was required to take two courses, Civics and American History. If I was successful in passing these courses, I would be eligible to take the GED test. I attended school at night and finished the two courses required.

In 1957 I took the GED test and passed, received my GED diploma, and was given the rank of Airman Second Class. I didn't realize at the time how important that GED diploma would become later in my life.

During my time in Spokane, I learned that not everyone was serious all the time. My first day at work was an eye opener. My sergeant told me to go on the flight line and get a bucket of prop wash. I grabbed a bucket and headed for the flight line. After going from one company to another and each one saying they were out of prop wash, they would send me to another place. I was finally stopped by the captain and asked who had sent me on that assignment. When I told him my sergeant, he said, "we'll see about that"!

What I didn't know at the time was that "prop wash" is the wind that flows alongside the airplane when the engines are running. It had all been a joke and everywhere I went they knew I was a raw recruit, so they would just go along with the gag and would send me to another shop. I don't know what happened to that sergeant, but I have never forgotten that "prop wash" is not something you can put in a bucket.

General Curtis Lamay, the SAC commander, made an inspection visit of our base in 1956. Everyone was jumping and running around, trying to make sure everything was in order.

When his plane arrived and he came down the stairs, a young airman assigned to the plane noticed he was smoking a cigar. He said to the general "Sir, you are not allowed to smoke near the airplane; it might catch on fire and blow up." Without missing a beat, General Lamay said, "It wouldn't dare".

During the cold war, B-36 bombers were the first strike deterrent for America, so we stayed on alert most of the time. After about a year in the state of Washington, I received orders to report to Andersen Air Force Base on the Island of Guam. My tour of duty was to be eighteen months. Actually, I was given my choice of duty. One year at Labrador Greenland, or eighteen months in Guam. I had enough of cold weather, so I opted for Guam. The climate in Guam is characterized as tropical marine, meaning hot and humid.

The average temperature is 86 degrees with an average annual rainfall of 98 inches.

Guam is the largest and southernmost island of the Mariana group. It's about 6,000 miles west of San Francisco. During the Second World War, Guam was attacked and invaded by the Japanese Army. It was under their control until the Battle of Guam, on July 21, 1944, when the United States recaptured it. To this day Guam remains the only U.S. soil ever to have been occupied by a foreign military power.

After the War, the United States established Guam as an unincorporated territory of the United States, and the people of Guam were granted U.S. citizenship. Andersen Air Force base is on the northern end of the island of Guam and sits atop a 500 ft plateau. The base was named for Brigadier General James Roy Andersen. It's since been changed, but when I was there, it was a Strategic Air Command base.

In 1951 five years before I arrived on Guam, the Strategic Air Command (SAC) chose several overseas bases to support its deployment of the B-29 bomber. In 1954 the B-29 was replaced with the B-36 bomber and the 3rd Air Division took control of operations. I arrived in early 1957 and was assigned to the 3960 Air Base Wing.

Additionally, the 41st Fighter–Interceptor Squadron of the Pacific Air Forces, along with its F-86s, was stationed at Andersen from August 1956 until several years after I had returned to the States.

During my tour of duty on Guam, I was privileged to visit several countries in the Far East. We flew supplies from Okinawa and Japan and were able to take R & R (Rest and Recuperation) from time to time. I spent time in the Philippines, Hong Kong, China, Japan, Okinawa, Johnson Island, and Hawaii.

On one trip to Japan, we were carrying among other things, strawberries for the Officers Mess. I made the trip on a transport plane from Guam to Yokota Air Base near Tokyo, Japan. On our return to Guam, we had just passed the point of no return when we lost an engine. With over 700 miles to go over the Pacific Ocean, the pilot sent out a May Day alert. He ordered us to lighten the airplane by throwing out everything that was not fixed to the plane. We opened the hatch and began throwing out everything in sight. The first thing to go was our cargo of strawberries.

We also were ordered to put on our parachutes and one-man dingy (a type of one-man lifeboat) and prepare to bail out. There were six of us not including the pilot and co-pilot, and we had practiced putting on our parachutes before we took off. It had taken about thirty minutes to get them on and ready, but now that we were about to jump, it only took a few minutes to get it all on.

With all the weight out of the plane, our descent began to slow, so the captain told us not to jump yet, he wanted to see if we could make it back to base on one engine. It was a harrowing few hours, just waiting to see if we were going to jump or not.

The captain told us to buckle up; he was going to try to make it to land. I watched as that little spec in the distance slowly became bigger and bigger, until I could make out the tip of the Island of Guam. We hit the runway with only a few feet to spare and the fire trucks had already foamed the runway and were waiting 95 for us. I don't remember praying, but looking back now, I'm sure I made contact, even though I didn't know with whom.

That was the first of two occasions when I was on an airplane that lost an engine. The other time was when I was returning to the states, and we lost an engine over the Pacific Ocean between Guam and Hawaii. We were able to land on Johnson Island where we spent a week waiting for a transport to bring us another engine. Both of those incidents were a little scary, but the Lord had his hand on me even back then.

After my tour of duty ended in the Pacific and it was time to return to the states, I was given my choice of bases where I could be stationed. I remember taking out a large United States map and looking at all the Air Force bases in the U.S. and thinking, "If I chose a base far from San Francisco, the Air Force will have to pay me travel going to that base and nine months later pay me travel to return to San Francisco". It was my idea to make as much money off Uncle Sam as possible. The base on the map that was the greatest distance from San Francisco was MacDill Air Force Base in Tampa, Florida, a base I didn't even know existed.

What I didn't know was that at the very same time I was making my decision, a young girl in Durant, Florida was praying and asking God to send her a Christian husband. She made a vow to God not to date any younger men unless they were born again. Of course, I was not born again and had no thought of becoming a Christian. Isn't it wonderful how God sometimes works in our lives even when we aren't aware of it?

My new car 1956 ford

CHAPTER 13
Going Stateside

I RETURNED TO California in December 1958. Since I had nowhere to live, I asked my brother Charles if I could stay with him for a couple of weeks until I left for my new base in Florida.

Charles had recently become a Christian and joined the Church of God. He was happy for me to stay with him and his wife, Joy, and his newborn daughter, Kim whom I loved from the moment I saw her. I named her "Ole Yeller" but believe me; the name had nothing to do with the movie "Ole Yeller".

I had been saving a little money while I was overseas and wanted to buy a car. I soon found out I couldn't borrow money to buy a car even though I had a down payment, and a steady job, because I had no credit rating. Charles agreed to co-sign for me, and I bought a 1956 Ford, baby blue and sharp as a tack. Looking back now I realize Charles was always there to take care of me when I needed him.

Charles and Joy began talking to me about becoming a Christian and I let them know that I was not interested. I was twenty years old and could not wait to become twenty-one so I could do whatever I wanted. They continued to pray for me for the next two weeks, but it didn't seem to do any good.

Charles told me later; he thought I was just too hard to ever come to the Lord. He didn't know it and I'm not sure I even knew it, but the Lord was beginning to work on me. I had money for a down payment only because I had part of my pay taken out and sent home to my Mama to save for me while I was overseas. She was determined that I would have money in the bank when I got back from overseas. She was tight fisted and wouldn't let me have any of it after she deposited it in the bank.

Once when I was in Japan on R. & R. and ran out of money, I sent her a telegram asking her to send me $100.00 of my own money. She sent a telegram back with one word saying "NO". I was glad when I got home and had saved enough money for a car, but at the time it made me so mad I could have shot her. After all it was my money and I needed it now!

After visiting my Daddy in Fresno and my Mama in Bakersfield, I left for Florida in my 1956 baby blue Ford Fairland. I have always been a country music fan (a flaw in my character) and my new car had an AM radio that played the best country music you could listen to.

As I traveled from California to Florida, I played the radio constantly. In the 1950's, as you traveled through Texas, Oklahoma, and the southern states, you could always find a country music station. The problem with those early AM stations was, they also had live gospel preachers. It seemed to me that every time I found a good music station, it wasn't long before some preacher would come on and preach Hell Fire and Brimstone. While I listened to those preachers on the radio, I came under heavy conviction. I began to make all kinds of promises to God and begged Him to leave me alone. One of those promises was that I would quit smoking if he would stop bothering me.

Smoking has always been a fascination to me. Even as a young person I always wanted to smoke. Everyone I knew growing up either smoked, dipped, or chewed tobacco. By the time I was six years old, I was smoking. I still remember the day I learned to inhale.

My cousin, Sammy Ansiel took me down in a basement on main street in Okmulgee, Oklahoma and taught me how to inhale. The first time I took a deep draw on that cigarette and filled my lungs with smoke I thought I was going to die.

I coughed and coughed but I kept on smoking and inhaling until it didn't hurt anymore and from that time on I was hooked. My habit became so bad, I was soon smoking two packs of cigarettes a day.

One of the worst whippings I ever got was when I stole some cigarettes from my Daddy as he slept. When he woke up and discovered his cigarettes were gone, he went looking for Charles and me. After he found us, he beat us with a wire shirt hanger until it broke in two. It didn't stop me from smoking, but it stopped me from stealing his cigarettes.

After turning off the radio and smoking my last pack of cigarettes, knowing I had made a vow to God, I decided to quit "cold turkey". It wasn't long before I wanted a smoke, bad! A two-pack addiction was hard to break, but I had made a vow to God that I wouldn't buy any more and I intended to keep it. Although I had decided not to buy anymore, that did not stop me from smoking everything I could find. First, I cleaned out the ashtray and smoked everything I could from there. When that was all gone, I pulled over to the side of the road and fumbled through the glove compartment until I found an old cigar that had been left there by the previous owner. I smoked that cigar until it burned my fingers to hold. After I threw that cigar butt out the window, I never smoked again. I've known people who have tried for years to quit smoking and have not been able to do so. For me, it was saying "that's it" and it was done, I never smoked again.

I've learned that smoking is a bad habit. It's not only unhealthy and expensive, but it affects others with its secondary smoke. It's hard for me to be around people who smoke now, but I remember I once was a smoker. When I arrived at MacDill Air Force Base in January 1959, I checked in with the officer of the day and was given a packet of information concerning the base and the surrounding area. In the packet was a booklet of churches, hospitals, restaurants, and other places of interest, as well as a Gideon New Testament. I pushed the bible back across the table and said, "This is one thing I don't need". The sergeant shoved it back and said, "take it anyway, it might come in handy".

In that packet of information was a listing of churches. Of course, they were listed alphabetically, and Assemblies of God churches were listed first. At that time in my life, I didn't know the difference between the Assemblies of God or any other denomination. For some reason the name Faith Tabernacle caught my attention. I had no idea what kind of church it was and didn't really care. There was no reason I should be interested in churches, but God was at work again and I didn't even know it.

A day or so after I had arrived at MacDill I decided to drive into town. I didn't realize it was Wednesday or that it even mattered, just that I wanted to get off the base for a while. As I drove off the base, I didn't have a clue as to where I was going, so I drove to the first stop sign, and turned right. After a few hundred yards I saw a church on my left, and I found myself turning into the parking lot. To this day I don't know why I turned into that churchyard. I hadn't been to church since I was a little boy in Oklahoma. Here I was sitting in the parking lot of Faith Tabernacle Assembly of God, Tampa, Florida.

After a few minutes I got out of the car and went inside the church. It was their Wednesday night prayer meeting, and there were only a handful of people. Since I didn't know the protocol of church gatherings, I sat down in the back of the church and waited. Just before the services started, a woman named Montez Green, approached me, and introduced herself as pastor.

She said, "We are so glad to have you tonight", and I said, "Thank you; I just love the God so much". I didn't even know what that meant; I was just trying to sound churchy. Looking back on that night, I know she must have seen through me the moment I opened my mouth.

As she returned to the front of the church, she asked everyone to join her at the altar for prayer before the service started. Everyone in the church got up and went to the altar. I looked around and realized I was the only one not at the altar. So as not to be conspicuous, I decided to join them. There are some people, who have seemingly been saved all their lives, and they can't really put their finger on the moment of their salvation, but I'm not one of them.

At an altar in a little church in Tampa, Florida, on Wednesday night January 7, 1959, I accepted Jesus as my personal Savior. I don't remember any fireworks, or bells, or angels singing, just the calm assurance that Jesus had forgiven me for my sins and had allowed me to become a child of God. From that moment on I have never doubted my salvation. Even when I strayed, I never doubted that He had forgiven me, and I belonged to Him.

I began to attend that church on Bay-to-Bay Ave., and the church family took me in, helped me to grow, and watched me mature into a believer. Jesus said, "Come unto me, all you who are weary and burdened, and I will give you rest. **(Matthew 11:28 NIV)**

Jesus was saying to me, "Olan, I know you are tired, burdened, and worn down. I see your broken heart, your shattered dreams, and your feeling of loneliness. I know you have lost your way, and you think your life has no real purpose. I will give you rest from all of that; I will show you the way".

That night I found my way. All my life I had been looking for something, and that something was Jesus, I just didn't know it. I will always have a great love for Pastor Montez

Green, and the Faith Tabernacle family, for being there for me when I first found the Lord.

After several weeks I met a young couple, Arthur and Martha Jo Cotton that attended the Faith Tabernacle. Arthur was also stationed at MacDill, and we became good friends. One day they asked me if I wanted to go with them to a "Speed the Light" service at their cousin's church in Durant, Florida. After telling me they were going to serve food, I agreed to go along.

I don't really remember much about the service, but I do remember the girl I met before the service that night. She was the prettiest girl I had ever seen, and she was asking me if I wanted something to drink. I couldn't keep my eyes off her! I know she must have felt uncomfortable with me staring at her all night.

On the way home that night I announced to my friends "I met the girl I'm going to marry!" When they asked me her name, I couldn't remember, but I couldn't forget her. I described her to them, and they decided it must have been Mary Lou Hinson.

Now the three most important things that ever happened in my life (Joining the Air Force, giving my life to Jesus, and finding the girl of my dreams) had already happened and I was only twenty years old!

Martha Jo and Mary Lou worked together at the First National Bank, and a few weeks after our trip to Pleasant Grove, my friends told me they were inviting Mary Lou to their home for dinner, and I was invited also if I wanted to come.

I could hardly wait for that day to come. What I didn't know was that they had not told Mary Lou I had also been invited. When Martha Jo and Mary Lou arrived, Arthur and I were in the swimming pool and invited them to join us. Mary

Lou put her hand over her eyes and informed me she didn't believe in "mixed bathing" and went inside the trailer.

Since I had only been saved a short time, and had missed out on the church's social rules, I had no idea what she was talking about. Even though I was such a novice, we somehow got through those first few hours. After Martha Jo and Arthur went to bed, we sat up and talked, and talked, and I fell in love.

A few days later some of Mary Lou's friends gave her a surprise birthday party and invited me to come. I don't know if the party was a surprise for Mary Lou but seeing me there certainly was. I knew Mary Lou was the girl for me, but my problem was convincing her.

I invited Mary Lou to join my friends Sergeant Henry Hudgins and his wife Ruth and me for a fishing trip off Gandy Bridge next week and she agreed. We didn't catch any fish, but we had a good time, and I was already beginning to win her heart.

I met Sergeant Henry Hudgins on my first day in Tampa, Florida. I was assigned to the helicopter supply area in hanger two, where he was the non-com in charge. Since I was new to the base, he took me under his wing. Henry invited me home for dinner and to meet his wife, Ruth. Ruth was a great cook, and I began to spend as much time as I could at their home. I had started attending Faith Tabernacle Assembly of God and I invited them to visit the church, which they did.

Henry was a professional Airman and spent the greater part of his life in the service of his country. After Mary Lou and I were married, they moved to Durant so we could be near each other.

For some odd reason, Henry called me "old destructive." It may have been because almost every time I went to their house, I broke something. I would reach to turn on a lamp and pull it over and break it. Or I would drop a glass, knock something over or find some other way to break something. Once when I was visiting Henry before he retired from the Air Force, he was showing me a new fishing lure and casting it out in the river and reeling it back in. I asked if I could cast it, and he said no! I might lose it or break it. I finally convinced him to let me try and on the first cast it landed high up in the branches of a tree growing on the riverbank. Needless to say, I broke the line trying to retrieve it. I suppose it's still hanging in that old tree. Ruth and Mary Lou became great friends and the years have only strengthened their friendship. We visit as often as we can, even though we live in different states.

I had dated a young girl from my church in Tampa a few times, but nothing serious. She played the guitar in church and was a wonderful Christian. I had told Sergeant Hudgins about her, and how she played the guitar, and sang. Henry told his wife Ruth, who also played the guitar and sang everything about her. Ruth looked forward to meeting her, since they had something in common.

I supposed I forgot all about that conversation, because a few weeks later, after I started dating Mary Lou. Henry and Ruth invited me for dinner at their house and asked me to bring this wonderful girl I was dating.

We had a nice dinner and then went to the living room for fellowship. A few minutes after we sat down, Ruth came in with a guitar, handed it to Mary Lou and asked her to play something. Mary Lou said she didn't play the guitar, but Ruth insisted and began telling her about how she had heard everything about her, and how beautifully she played the guitar and sang. The bad thing about all this was Mary Lou knew the other girl. I had a lot of explaining to do to get out of that one!

After several dates, we were going home one Sunday afternoon after a gospel sing, and I asked her when she was going to go with me to my church in Tampa. She replied, "I'm not going to go with you to your church because, I am not going to date you anymore." Well, I said, "I'm going to keep asking, so you will just have to refuse." I don't think she ever refused.

She was five feet nine inches tall, and I was only five feet eight inches tall in my cowboy boots, I think she was a little self-conscious at her height, but I didn't let that stop me. I did promise to carry a little stool around to stand on if she wanted me too, but she never took me up on that, thank goodness! My car soon came in handy, because one evening while I was lying on my bunk in the barracks, I was told I had a call in the dayroom. It was Mary Lou; she was at work at the First National Bank of Tampa and had worked overtime and had no way home. She lived in Durant, Florida about 25 miles from Tampa. She asked me if I could give her a ride home, and of course I said "yes". Little did she know that this was going to be the start of something great!

I was persistent and continued to ask her to go out for a date. Even though she said she didn't want to date me, she often had the problem of getting a ride home from work. I was always ready to hop in my car and head for the bank where she worked.

Living on Air Force pay meant that most of the time I was short on money, so I started selling some of my personal items to get a few dollars. I went through my sunglasses, my extra hats, my extra fatigues, my watch, my ring and even took KP duty to earn extra money.

Mary Lou and Me at our first home.

CHAPTER 14
Finding a Good Thing

FOR THE NEXT several months I saw Mary Lou every night either to take her home after work, or to take her to church, or just show up at her house and just say "hello", "here I am". By the time summer was over, I had worn down her resistance and began asking her to become my wife. For reasons known only to God, she said "yes"!

I wanted to buy her an engagement ring, but I didn't have any money or credit. When I told her my predicament, she said she had a charge account at the Duval Jewelry Store in Tampa, and if I wanted to use it, I could put it on her charge account. I don't remember how she got it approved with the store, but the next day I went to Duval's and picked out her ring. The total cost was $100.00, including tax and I put it in her charge account. (I paid her back that $100.00, on our 50th wedding anniversary).

When I picked her up from the bank, we walked to the parking lot and before I started the car, I opened that little box and gave her the ring (she cried). I took her home and she showed her ring to her mother. Mama Hinson was happy for her but had mixed feeling because she hated to see Mary Lou get married and maybe move away, since she was marrying a man from California. We went to show her sister Evelyn her ring and she was happy for us and invited us to stay for dinner. That's a tradition we still enjoy.

There are so many times that God came to my rescue during those days. I remember a time when after church one Sunday night, Mary Lou wanted to go to the Sunny South drive-in for a hamburger. I only had a few dollars that I was going to use to put gas in my car in order to get back to base, but I couldn't say no.

Mary Lou had no idea I was broke, so she invited her girlfriends, Andrea Maute, and Connie Martin, to go along with us. All three of them ordered a hamburger, fries, and coke, and then asked me "what are you going to get?" I barely had enough money to pay for theirs, so I told them I was not hungry, which was the truth because now I was sick to my stomach, worrying about having enough gas to get these girls home. Eating was the last thing on my mind.

For the first time in my young Christian life, I began to pray for a miracle. I kept my eye on the gas gage that was now below empty. I asked God to let me get these girls home and then I would happily run out of gas and walk all the way to MacDill Air Force Base for help.

I continued to pray as each one of them was dropped off at their home. When I finally got to Mary Lou's house, she asked me if something was wrong, because I had hardly spoken a word all the way home. It's hard to talk when you are praying, so I just said, "I'm not feeling well." As I left her house that night, I started praising God for His miracle of putting gasoline in my car.

I said, "OK, God, you can let me run out of gas now! It's all right. I'm ready to walk now," I couldn't believe that my car was still going. With the gage empty from Plant City to Bloomingdale, and back to Durant, there was no way I had enough gas to cross the street, let alone go back to MacDill Air Force Base.

As I drove along that night praising God and waiting any moment to run out of gas, I learned "All things are possible if you only believe", and I got all the way back to the base without running out of gas!

On another miraculous occasion I was playing volleyball with the youth one night at church, when I noticed Mary Lou's class ring that she had given me was gone. Somehow it had slipped off my finger while we were playing and was buried under the sand. I told Mary Lou I had lost her ring and we both looked for it, but to no avail. Again, I started praying for a miracle.

The next day before I went to her house to pick her up, I went back to the volleyball court praying all the way. When I got out of my car, I walked to a spot in the sand and looked down. There in the sand was her ring right where God had shown me to look.

The lesson I learned in these two miracles is that God is not only interested in the "Big" things; but that He is also interested in those little things that touch our lives.

Mary Lou and I planned to get married after I was discharged from the Air Force in September because I would not be twenty-one until September 3rd, 1959, and would not be able to get married without my parent's signature, but I knew that was not going to happen. We set the date for October 2, 1959, one month after my twenty-first birthday.

There was a time when I didn't know if the wedding would take place or not. Mary Lou's brothers asked me if I wanted to go cast net fishing with them. I didn't even know what cast net fishing was, but I was about to find out. Fishing for mullet in the Alafia River is a past time that all her brothers were proficient at. It is usually done from a "Jon Boat", where someone will guide the boat, and another will throw a cast net. A Jon or "John" boat is a flat bottom boat used in shallow and still waters like a lake, pond, or shallow river. A good cast netter can make the net fan out like a silver dollar while catching as many as two dozen fish at a time. As you drift along looking for mullet as they jump out of the water while schooling and looking for food, you throw the cast net and then pull in your catch. Occasionally, your boat runs up on a sandbar and you must jump out and push it off. From time to time, we would run up on a sandbar and Talmadge, Alton, or Earl, would jump out and push us off. As we were slowly moving down the mouth of the river, the boat suddenly stopped and Earl said "Olan, jump out and push us off the sandbar". Even though I was not dressed for fishing, I jumped out of the boat in what I thought was very shallow water. What I didn't know was that we were in the middle of the river and the water was over ten feet deep. I remember wearing a new fedora and as I came out of the water, I watched it float away. Those brothers of Mary Lou didn't know if I would sink or swim, but they knew how to laugh. I thought about just getting out and going to the airport and catching a flight to California, but then I decided not to blame Mary Lou for her crazy brothers.

We were married at Pleasant Grove Assembly of God, Durant Florida, on Friday night October 2, 1959, by Pastor C.C. Garrett. We spent the first night of our Honeymoon, at the Siesta Motel in Zephyrhills, Florida. Mary Lou's brother Talmadge, and some of his friends had followed us in a caravan and harassed us all the way. We thought we had lost them and pulled into the motel for the night. After checking in, we looked around and there they were pulling up behind our car. They had locked a chain of tin cans to the bumper of our car. After giving us a hard time, they said they had lost the key and couldn't unlock the chain. After a little more harassing, they said they would unlock the chain and leave us alone, so we ran to our room and locked ourselves in for the night. We discovered the next morning we had left the key in the door all night!

The next morning, we drove to Ocala, Florida and stayed at the Hotel Ocala. They asked if we were newlyweds, I guess we looked the part. That afternoon we visited Silver Springs and went out on the famous Glass Bottom boat. Someone asked us as we boarded our boat for a trip up the river, how long we had been married and we said, "Two whole days", and everyone laughed. Sunday, we returned to our home in Durant, Florida. It was a small two-bedroom frame house on Blount Road. We were thrilled to be living in our own home.

A few weeks before we were married, I learned that Eugene Blount had a house he wanted to sell, along with one acre of land on Blount Road. It was his old house, and he wanted to move to Lakeland, Florida. He was asking $2,500.00 for it and it was a good buy. The only problem was I didn't have that amount of money, even with my discharge payout. So, we went to the bank and applied for a loan. They asked me how much I had for a down payment, and I said "nothing". They said I had to pay down 10% of the purchase price, which I didn't have.

When I told Eugene, he said "no problem"; I'll ask $3500.00 for the purchase for the house and give you a thousand dollars as a wedding present. The bank agreed to loan us the money to buy the house, and we moved into our first house the day we returned from our honeymoon.

All the family of Charles, Mary, and me

CHAPTER 15
Family

O FTEN THINK of not having a family when I was growing up, and how I missed being a part of a loving family. Since I never had much of a family life; I really didn't know what I missed. I do know that God made up for all that by giving me not only a wonderful family with Mary Lou and our children, Holli, Doyle, and Chuck, but he also gave me a huge church family.

While Mary Lou and I were dating, the first members of my new God given family, was the Cotton family, Elsie, Murray, Dickie, and Martha. Dickie and Martha became as close to me as my own siblings. And Elsie was like a mother to me, and even stood in for my mother who couldn't come to our wedding. Every Sunday after church I would go to the Cotton house for Sunday dinner. No one could make fried cornbread or fried okra like Elsie. After dinner we played croquet or sat around and talked about what happened at church or took a nap (a Pentecostal tradition). Sometimes they would make homemade ice cream and play other games. I owe so much of my early Christian training to Elsie's guiding hand. Elsie was always taking care of us in one way or another.

Once when we were starting on a trip to California, Elsie ran out to our car and handed Mary Lou a new pair of shoes. She knew we didn't have much money and she just wanted to be a blessing. Often, she would see to it that we had something to eat, either by bringing something to our house, and leaving it on the table, or just inviting us to eat with them.

One night after a revival meeting at church, I invited a couple from Bible College, home for coffee and snacks only to realize we didn't have any snacks to offer. When Elsie overheard me talking to them at church, she rushed home, got a plate of cookies, and took it over to our house before we returned from church. When we walked in, we knew an angel had been in our house and left us something to serve our guest.

Murray and Elsie were always there to help and encourage me in my new walk with the Lord. Even though I was fairly new to their lives, they loved me and welcomed me into their family. Elsie and Murray knew I was an old piece of coal, but they also knew if God could just get through to me, He might be able to use me.

Another family that God gave me in those early days was the Albert Martin family. Albert and Wilma Martin, lived in Durant, just a short distance from Pleasant Grove Assembly of God, and had lived in the area for most of their lives.

Albert was a great man and one of the finest Christian men I have ever known. He wasn't so spiritual minded that he was no earthly good. He was practical, wise, loving and giving. Over the years I learned to love him like a father, like the one I never had. Wilma was one of the most precious women I ever knew, who was also kind, loving, giving, and always ready to help.

I stayed at their house more than I did at my own, partly because I liked to be around them and partly because they always insisted on my staying to eat. If someone was looking for me, the first place they would call was Albert Martin's home. I think God was trying to give me the family I never had, and He was doing a great job of it.

After I had graduated from Southeastern Bible College, Mary Lou and I became Children and Youth Evangelists traveling during the summer. One of Albert and Wilma's daughters (Marlene), traveled with us, played the piano, and sang at our services. She was a wonderful singer and greatly anointed by God. The first church I pastored was Sydney Assembly of God, and it was because of Albert, I became the pastor.

During a revival I was conducting in Winter Garden Assembly of God in Orlando, Florida, three men came to visit and sat down in the back of the church. They were deacons for Sydney Assembly of God and were without a pastor. I didn't know it, but they were there to look me over.

After church that night, one of them asked Mary Lou how she would like to be the wife of the next pastor of Sydney. She answered, "It depends on who he is". I don't know what they saw in me that would make a good pastor but after the service that night they asked if I would accept their offer to become their pastor. I accepted and had the joy of leading my first church.

Albert loved to sing and was the song leader at our church for several years. I will never forget the times we would all gather around the old upright piano, with Martha playing the piano and the rest of us singing. We could stay around that old upright piano for what seemed like hours. Martha, Mary Lou, and I formed the "Sydney Trio" and sang those old time Southern Gospel songs. I wouldn't say we were good, but we didn't run anyone off.

I was pastor of Sydney Assembly of God for ten years. Those years of pastoring at Sydney were the greatest years of our ministry. When we resigned the pastorate, our congregation had grown to a full house, and we were in the process of looking for property to build a new church. Resigning was one of the hardest things I ever did, but I knew it was time.

After resigning the church in Sydney, I became the associate pastor of Pleasant Grove Assembly of God. I served as the associate pastor with Pastor Hubert Wallace and remained in that position for the next five or six years, until pastor Wallace resigned. I became the interim pastor, for about six months until the church called Rev. Donald Jolley, of Macon, Georgia, to be pastor. I became his associate and remained in that position with the church for the next five years.

Pleasant Grove Assembly of God has always been my home church. Even when I was a pastor elsewhere, I still thought of Pleasant Grove as my home church. Mary Lou and I were married there, Holli, and Marvin were married there, and Heidi our granddaughter was married there. That was the last special event ever held in the old church before it was torn down.

A building is not the church, I know that, but it is the place where the church meets to encourage one another, and to show Christ to the world. It's made up of people and that's why I love Pleasant Grove Assembly of God, a place where so many good people go and so many good things happened to me.

CHAPTER 16
The Swimming Pool Incident

SEVERAL YEARS AFTER we were married we had a swimming pool installed at our home in Sydney. One day I noticed the pool was leaking a small amount of water every day. As I looked down into the pool, I noticed a small crack in the bottom. I purchased a repair kit from the local pool supply store and geared up to repair it. I rolled the two types of adhesives together to create the bonding material and jumped into the pool, only to realize I could not stay on the bottom of the pool long enough to repair the crack.

I decided I needed something heavy enough to keep me down on the bottom long enough to repair the crack. As I looked around, I spotted Doyle's weightlifting set at the end of the pool. I selected a twenty-five-pound weight and stuffed it into the webbing of my swimsuit. I didn't want it to come out at the bottom of the pool, so I tied the knot, tight enough to keep it in. Now I was ready to stay down long enough to repair the crack.

I jumped off the side of the pool and immediately descended to the bottom. I thought this is great, now I have time to fix the crack without having to keep swimming to stay on the bottom. I worked for several minutes and realized I was out of air. Now it was time to return to the top and get another breath. As I tried to swim to the surface, I realized I weighed too much in the seat of my pants and that I had better get that weight out of my swimsuit. Frantically I started to untie the string and suddenly found out that wet string is hard to untie at the bottom of a pool. The string would not untie, and I could not swim with twenty-five pounds of steel in my swimsuit. A million things went through my mind as I began to lose consciousness. What will people think? Will they think I committed suicide? Will they think I was exercising? or will they just think, what a dumb idea he had.

As my air ran out, I panicked, my lungs began to burn, my legs could not lift me off the floor of the pool and I could not disengage the weight. As a last resort, I fell to the bottom of the pool and slowly crawled to the side where the ladder was.

At the very last moment I reached up and caught the bottom rung and pulled myself up to the top for a gasp of air. Thank God for being there when you need Him.

My Lloyd car

CHAPTER 17

My Cars

Lloyd

DURING MY SECOND year of Bible College, I decided to earn money by taking a paper route. It was to deliver the evening edition of the Tampa Times. Since I wanted a car with good gas mileage, I bought a two-door, four cylinders, 1950 Lloyd. This was a small German car and had absolutely no resemblance to the German carmaker Mercedes Benz.

After a few weeks of delivering the paper, the starter on the Lloyd broke and I began a search to replace it. After an exhausting search, I found the only way to get a new starter was to order it from the Lloyd Company in Germany. Since I didn't have the money to get it fixed, I decided to go without a starter and every time I wanted to start it, I would have to push it to start. It was very light and usually didn't take much of a push to get it going.

At night I parked it out by the road where there was a small incline. In the morning I would get in, take the break off, and let it roll down the little incline, put it in gear and let off on the clutch. It would start and off I would go. I drove to college and would park in the parking lot where I could push it without too much trouble, then jump in and start it. I learned not to shut it off, unless I was going to be parked for some time, because it was not always easy to find a good spot where I could push it off.

On Easter Sunday, 1961 Larry Rice, a young man from my church and I decided to go to Lake Wales, for an Easter Sunrise service with the Rev. Billy Graham. It wasn't any trouble getting the Lloyd started to make the trip, but coming back was a different story. When we parked in the parking lot at the outdoor stadium, we didn't have any idea we wouldn't have enough room to start our car. When the service was over, Larry and I went to get the car to come home, knowing that we would have to push it to get it started. The only trouble was that every time we got enough room between us and the car in front, we would start pushing and before we could jump in and start it, another car would pull out in front of us, and we would have to stop and try again. After several failed attempts we decided to wait until all the cars left the parking lot so we would have enough room to get our car started. We didn't make it in time for church at Pleasant Grove Assembly of God that Sunday.

I sold that Lloyd a few years later, and it still didn't have a starter.

English Ford

Our next car was an English Ford, probably the best car I ever owned. It was new when we bought it and we loved it. Not too long after we got it, Mary Lou and her sister were going to a wedding in Tampa. My Sister-in-law, Sharon had just gotten her driver's license and was driving my new car to her brother's wedding, when she turned in front of an oncoming car. The car hit the back fender of my beautiful English Ford and made a large dent. The Insurance Company sent us a check for the repair, and we decided we would just keep the check and not fix the car until later, since we needed the money more than we needed the repair. We drove that car with the bent fender for over a year and of course, we had already spent the insurance money.

Sometime later my good friend Albert said he had seen a car just like the one I had, in a junkyard and the right rear fender was in good shape. Albert said, "If you want me to, I can cut the old fender off and weld the new fender on, and it will look good as new." I bought the fender from the junkyard and carried it to him so he could cut the old one off and weld the new one on. It took him several days, but when he finished, he called me to come get it. When I looked at it, it was a great job, I thought all it needed was to be painted. However, after a closer look we discovered that I had bought the wrong fender. The right fender rear light was turned sideways, and the left fender rear light, went straight up and down. It reminded me of a song I had heard by Johnny Cash about a Cadillac he put together, one piece at a time.

So much for my cars.

Mary Lou, Holli, Doyle, Chuck, and me in front of Sydney Assembly of God

CHAPTER 18

Taking Mary Lou to California

AFTER MARY LOU and I married, she started a great relationship with my mother who lived in Bakersfield, California. They began to correspond and after a couple of years we decided to visit them. It was over 3000 miles from Florida to California and we didn't have air conditioning in our car. We made the trip in July because we had to go during summer vacation. I told Mary Lou that this trip would take us to heaven. If we made it to California we would be in heaven, and if something happened to us and we were killed, we would be in heaven, so either way we would end up in heaven. It was a hot, miserable trip, with no air conditioning and when we reached Death Valley, the temperature was 110 degrees. Mary Lou turned, looked at me and said, "Honey, I think you took a wrong turn and we've ended up in that other place".

Going over the mountains was hot and put a strain on the engine. Somewhere on top of one of these huge ridges, my radiator hose exploded, and I had to pull over and stop. Mary Lou and I didn't know what to do, so we began to pray. Now how could God do anything on top of a mountain?

After praying for a short time, I got out of the car and began walking down the ditch on the side of the road. As I walked along praying, I looked down and there in the ditch was a radiator hose. I picked it up and examined it to see if there was anything wrong with it. There was not so much as a pinhole in it, and it was a perfect fit for the car. I removed the old one and replaced it with a new one. I looked back in that ditch and there was a pool of water that held enough water to fill my radiator. This was just another little miracle on which to build my faith.

Another time we wanted to visit my Mama, but we didn't have enough money, so Albert said he would pay for the gas if we took him and Wilma along as far as Beaumont, Texas. So, with $100.00, and Albert's Shell Oil Credit Card, we headed for Texas, and California. The trip went without incident, but the return was a different story.

After two weeks with my family in California, we started on our return to Florida. The day before we left, I had the car serviced and when they put on the oil filter, they put it on cross-threaded, so the oil had slowly been dripping out. As we left, mother had fixed a box of food to take with us, including her delicious fried chicken. She was a great cook, and we were thankful for the "food to go". Just before we reached Santa Rosa, New Mexico, the red light on the dash came on, and I was asleep in the back seat. Since Mary Lou didn't know what the red light meant she continued to drive. As the engine began to knock Mary Lou grew concerned and woke me. Before I could stop the car, I heard a loud noise, and the car came to a stop on the side of old route 66. I flagged down a truck and asked the driver if he would pull us into the nearest town, which was Santa Rosa, New Mexico. We found out the engine had thrown a rod and cracked the side of the block. The whole engine had to be replaced. The replacement of an engine was out of the question since I didn't have nearly enough money.

We were stretched very thin, with little money of our own, and only Albert's credit card to get back us back home. In those days credit card companies would only let you pay for gas and maybe a candy bar or coke. I decided the best thing to do was to call Albert. Mary Lou wanted me to call my Mama or Daddy and ask them to help, but I had never asked them for anything before, and I wasn't going to start now. I called Albert and he said he would think of something, to wait and he would call me back.

When he called me back, he had a plan. His nephew, Vernon Baggett, was in the Air Force and stationed just a few miles from Clovis, New Mexico. He had a pick-up truck parked in his backyard and offered to let me borrow it. Vernon was visiting with his mother "Cookie" in Beaumont, Texas, and that's where Albert and Wilma were visiting as well. With only a few dollars left, I decided to buy a ticket back to Clovis, New Mexico and then buy another ticket from Clovis, to the Air Force Base to get the truck. We had decided it would be best for Mary Lou to wait at the bus station in Santa Rosa until I could get the truck and return it the next day. The only problem was the bus station closed at 6:00 PM and she would not be allowed to stay. We had to buy another ticket for her to go with me and that took the last money we had. We paid for our tickets and were on our way. Around midnight we got off the bus and were told the Air Base was about a mile off the road. It was pitch dark with no moonlight, but we started to walk down the road toward the base.

When we got near the base, I could see a trailer park on the right. Vernon had said, "His truck was green and would be on the right parked under an awning, and the key would be under the floor mat." As we looked down the road into the trailer park, virtually every trailer had a truck parked under an awning, and several of them were green. Vernon had said he thought his trailer was the third or fourth on the left after we came in the park. Although we had no way of knowing which truck was his, we decided to try to open the door on one and look under the floor mat to see if we could find a key. Sure, the first one we tried was a green truck under an awning and had a key under the floor mat. As we started the truck and drove away, I told Mary Lou to look in the glove compartment and see if we could find anything to prove to us we had the right truck. When she opened the glove compartment, she saw a letter and pulled it out to read. It was addressed to Mr. James Smith. I said "Oh! No, we have stolen someone's truck!" She frantically searched through the glove compartment and gave a sigh of relief as she said, "Here's a letter addressed to Mr. Vernon Baggett."

We drove to Santa Rosa to pick up my car, and with an old chain Vernon had in the back of the truck, we chained our car to the bumper of Vernon's truck and began to pull our car from New Mexico to Texas and then to Florida. We ate what we had left of Mama's fried chicken, and from then on it was only gas and candy bars with Albert's credit card.

Even though Mary Lou had never steered a car while it was being pulled, she quickly learned. After a few hours, the battery on the car ran down and from then on, we had no lights or horns on the car. We drove to the next large town and had a towbar made so we could both ride in the truck and pull the car behind. We drove during the day and would park in a lighted area during the night and sleep in the car. I think the happiest day of my life was when I pulled up in front of the house where Albert and Wilma were staying.

The next day we loaded everything in the back of the truck and in the trunk of the car and started for Florida. Even though Mary Lou didn't have to steer the car, it was still very unnerving for the ladies to ride without any communication whatsoever with us in the truck. Since they had no power in the car, they could not even blow the horn to get our attention.

As we traveled around some narrow and very dangerous roads the car began to swerve and sway back and forth. Before we could get it stopped, it jack-knifed, and we slid down the road toward a deep ravine. Just before we went over the side both the truck and car came to a stop. It was as if an angel had put out his hand and stopped us.

When we neared the city of New Orleans, we passed a cemetery on our right and I remarked to Albert, that there was a huge statue of Jesus in the middle of that cemetery. It was quite a sight, and it must have been thirty to forty feet high. We had to follow the road signs through New Orleans, and it was very confusing to drive and try to follow the signs, while pulling our car behind us, but I finally got through. As we traveled several miles on the other side of New Orleans, I noticed another cemetery this time on our left. It also had a large statue of Jesus, and I pointed it out to Albert that they had a cemetery on both sides of New Orleans that were just alike.

Albert threw up his hands and said, "You dummy, you have driven into New Orleans, turned around, and now we are headed back the same way we came."

I will always be grateful to Vernon Baggett, my friend, of almost 50 years, for his kind and generous spirit in allowing us to use his truck.

Holli, Mary Lou and me

CHAPTER 19
Call to Ministry

C AMP MEETING WAS always a great time at Pleasant Grove Assembly of God. Ten days of preaching, praying, singing, and spending time around the altar after service. It was a tradition to go every night, because if you missed one night that would be the very night something special would happen.

In 1959 shortly after camp meeting, Pastor Garrett asked Rev. Edward Blount, a Missionary to the Philippines, to conduct a revival at Pleasant Grove. It was a great time in the Lord, and on the last night of the revival Brother Blount preached a sermon titled "But if not." The title of course comes from Daniel Chapter 3 verse 18, a well-known chapter about the three Hebrew children when they were thrown into the fiery furnace. At the end of his message, he challenged us to give ourselves completely to God for His use. That was a night I will never forget. I remember almost everything that happened in that service. Many people went to the altar to pray, and many were touched by the power of God. After a long while, the altar service was coming to a close and everyone was returning to their seats, but I was having a private conversation with God. He was speaking to my heart and telling me He wanted me to go to Bible College. I spent the better part of an hour arguing with Him. I gave Him every excuse I could muster up; I don't have a high school diploma,

I don't have the money for Bible College, I just got married, I'm not smart enough for college, and so on. All of my excuses were legitimate as any rational person could see. God, however, is not rational as we think of being humanly rational. To each of my objections He simply said, "I'll make a way".

The next morning, I asked Roland Blount, my brother-in-law, to go with me to Southeastern Bible College in Lakeland, Florida to see about enrolling in Bible College. When we arrived on campus, we went to the office and a young lady greeted us and asked if she could help us. I told her about my encounter with the Lord and I would like to enroll in Bible College. She explained to me that they were in the middle of the semester, and I would have to wait until the semester ended before I could enroll. I didn't know much about college, but I knew God had spoken to me and had told me to go. At that time, I began to wonder if this was the right place for me. After all, if this was a real Bible College that listened to God, wouldn't they know I was supposed to be here? Somebody was missing God, and it wasn't me, or so I thought. Even though I was very disappointed, I returned home and waited until the end of the semester before enrolling.

Mary Lou and me headed to South-Eastern Bible College

CHAPTER 20
College

FOR A BOY from Oklahoma, with a ninth grade education, the idea of going to college was about as far from reality as you could get. I knew I did not belong, but God had called me and told me to go to Bible College. Through all the years, I never doubted my call. I wondered at God's wisdom, but never doubted the call.

In January 1960 I enrolled in Southeastern Bible College, now South-eastern University. Since I had not finished high school and didn't have a diploma, I was allowed to use my GED diploma. I will always be grateful to my Air Force commanding officer years earlier who practically ordered me to get my GED. Even though I was allowed to enroll, I still was required to take several extra classes to help me with my core courses. College was not easy for me, and I had to learn how to study. I spent long hours reading chapters over and over, just to try to understand what they were saying. Although I knew I wasn't very smart, I didn't want anyone else to know, so I listened a lot and tried not to talk much.

During one of my first classes the professor continued to use a word I had never heard. He said we would have to turn in a written "hypothesis" on the subject. I didn't have a clue what "hypothesis" was, but I wasn't going to raise my hand and ask, so I waited to hope there was someone in the class as dumb as me. Sure enough, a young man in the back of the class raised his hand and asked what the word "hypothesis" meant. I noticed a few students snickering and I was glad I had not been the one to show my ignorance.

School was hard and even though I studied and studied, I just didn't get it! After a few weeks into the semester, we were told we would be having a test the next day in my General Science class. That night I studied hard and spent most of the night trying to learn all I could. The next morning, I went to class as confidently as I could, knowing I had studied and was ready for the test. When the test paper was handed out, the teacher said, "when you have finished, just bring your test up and lay it on my desk and you may leave."

When I turned the test over and began to look it over, I was dumbfounded. I went up and down the test and began to panic. I realized I did not know the answer to a single question. The only thing I knew was the space that said, "Name". I couldn't believe it, I had read the chapter repeatedly, yet I did not see anything on the test I was even vaguely familiar with. After being in college for over three weeks, I was still as dumb as the day I enrolled. I was too embarrassed to admit to anyone that I didn't know any of the answers, so I kept my head down and filled in some letters with my pen. I waited until several students had finished their test and placed them on the desk and left before I handed in my test.

When I finally decided to take my paper up, I turned it upside down on the others and headed for the door. All the while I was praying and telling myself if I could just get to my car and get off this campus, Southeastern would not have to bother with me again. I wasn't college material, and if God wanted me to preach, He would just have to use me without an education.

As I closed the door behind me, I headed down the hall as fast as my feet would take me. Just as I reached for the exit door hoping to escape, I heard a voice behind me calling my name. "Mr. Hill" The voice said, "Wait just a moment please".

I froze, knowing that I was about to face my humiliation head on. The voice belonged to Dr. Thomas Wilson, professor of General Science. As he approached, I could feel the blood rushing to my face and knew he was about to tell me I didn't belong in his class. To my utter surprise, he was very kind and gentle. He said, "I noticed you didn't answer any of the test questions, is there a reason for that?" he asked. Well, it's too late now to try to fool anyone, I thought, so I answered as best I could. "The reason" I said was "I didn't know any of the answers on the test". "Didn't you study?" He asked "Oh! Yes, I studied" I said, "but nothing I studied was on the test".

Then he said something I will never forget; "Now you think you aren't smart enough for college and you have decided to quit, haven't you?" How did he know that? That was exactly what I was thinking. He put his hand on my shoulder and said, "don't do that, if God has called you here, He hasn't changed his mind." "Give us another chance to help you, I know you have been out of school a long time, been in the service and probably have forgotten how to study." I hadn't forgotten how to study; I had never learned how to study. That moment in time changed my life forever. Dr. Thomas Wilson will always be the greatest teacher I ever knew.

I did decide to return the next day, and Dr. Wilson helped me to learn how to study; to look for the important idea in the beginning paragraph, and to memorize those things that were important. Dr. Wilson taught me how to outline, and write short paraphrases, to find those items that were important and those that were not, and how to stay on task. His techniques have been a help to me all through my years as a student and teacher.

Oh! And by the way I did pass his General Science class at the end of the semester, I am happy to announce I received a "D" in that class. It was probably a higher grade than I really deserved, but I was thankful for it. Dr. Thomas was also correct when he said, "If God has called you, He will see you through."

There are far too many incidents during those years to tell but a few sticks out in my memory. About a year of going to school and trying to work little jobs just to pay the bills, we came to a place in our lives where we were down to our last dime and were already behind on our tuition. It looked as though I would have to drop out of college, because we simply couldn't pay our bills. Mary Lou was working full-time and doing the best she could, but it wasn't enough to pay all the bills and pay for college too. All we could do was pray. I had tried to work part time when I could, but work was hard to come by and didn't bring in enough money to help much. I worked at Nichol's Mine Co. the summer before, on a part time basis but that only lasted a couple of months and then I was laid off. I applied for summer work again and was told that there were no jobs available.

Wednesday night before I had to make my decision, Mary Lou and I went to church very down and discouraged and feeling like there was no way out this time. I don't really remember much from the service except on that night the pastor asked if anyone had a testimony. It was not unusual for a Wednesday night service to have a testimony time, but this time the testimony seemed to be for Mary Lou and me. One of the elderly ladies of the church Sister Minnie Woolridge testified about how good God had been to her, but it was the end of her testimony that ministered to us. She said, "God will meet your need, even if He has to rain dollar bills down from heaven." Both of us felt that God was going to meet our need, and all we had to do was trust Him.

The next day I was visiting with my good friend Albert Martin, when his wife called from the house and said I had a phone call from the personnel director of Nichol's mine. He had made three long distance calls to find me that day. First, he called my house, and of course Mary Lou was working, and I was gone. Next, he called the number of my Mother-in-law, which I had given on the application, and she said I was not there, but she gave him Albert's number and so he called there.

When I answered the phone, I was a little disappointed when he said he had noticed on my application I was looking for a part time job during the summer. He went on to say that he was sorry that he didn't have any summer jobs available but was wondering if I would be interested in a full-time job. The only problem was that the job he had available was working from 2:00 PM until 10:00 PM, Monday through Friday. I don't remember shouting much through the years, but this was one time I really felt like shouting.

It was perfect, because I got out of school every day at noon and that gave me time for lunch and the drive to Mulberry to start work at 2:00 PM. I worked there for the next three years in the chemistry lab. I would check in and take the lab truck out to the mining areas and gather samples of phosphate rock. After gathering the samples and returning to the lab, I would prepare them for the lab technician's next day's analysis. I usually finished work about 8:00 PM, and then had two hours of my shift left that I was allowed to use for study.

Over the years I have been reminded of those encouraging words of Sister Minnie Woolridge, who said "God will rain dollar bills down from heaven if He has too, to meet your needs." He didn't rain dollar bills down from heaven to meet our needs, but He did provide me with a good job that lasted until I finished Bible College.

I graduated from Southeastern Bible College in 1963. Mary Lou bought me a Thompson chain reference bible, for my graduation, which I still have. It was one of the greatest gifts I ever received. To this day I don't know where she got the money for it. She must have saved a long time.

My first job after graduation was teaching fifth grade at Pinecrest Elementary School, in East Hillsborough County, Florida. After one year at Pinecrest, I transferred to Dover Elementary and taught there for the next six years. During the summer of my second year of teaching at Dover Elementary, Mary Lou and I became children's evangelists and traveled around the country conducting "Kids Krusades" and "Youth Revivals".

After teaching for several years at Dover, I enrolled at Rollin's College in Winter Park, Florida, and graduated with a Master's Degree in Administration and Supervision.

After receiving my Master's Degree, I was asked to become the Principal of Clair-Mel Elementary School. At that time, it was the largest elementary school in Hillsborough County with over 1200 students.

After a few years, I transferred and became Principal of Philip Shore Sixth Grade Center in Tampa, Florida. I remained there until I retired in 1996, after 33 years of service to the Hillsborough County School system.

Dad, with Charles, Wayne, and me

CHAPTER 21

Forgiveness

OVER THE YEARS I have heard a lot about the need for forgiveness. For years, I felt as though I had been abused by a father and mother, who didn't care about me. As I grew older, I tried to understand how a mother or father could be so unconcerned about their children that they could give them away. How they could bring them into this world and then not want them.

With God's help, I have learned to forgive. In the bible, the book of Matthew (6:14-15) NIV says, "For if you forgive men when they sin against you, your heavenly Father will also forgive you. But if you do not forgive men their sins, your Father will not forgive your sins."

I recently saw a news item that was a follow up on a shooting that had happened a year before. An innocent woman was shot in the crossfire between two men. She became paralyzed by the injury. The thing that struck me most was her statement: "I haven't forgiven them yet, but I know I have to, because if I don't forgive them, God won't forgive me."

If I have learned anything about my early years of growing up, it is this: If I want God to forgive me, I must forgive others.

Some people have trouble with forgiveness, and I supposed for a long time I did also. Growing up I had a lot of anger toward my Daddy and Mama. I never looked at the circumstances of their own lives. Neither of them had much education or instruction on how to raise children. The whole meaning in their lives was how to just get through the day! For years I thought I would forgive them one day when they came to me and asked for forgiveness. But that's not God's way, He says, "I forgive you, now you forgive others".

In his book "What's so Amazing About Grace," Philip Yancey tells a story about a man and wife who one night had an argument about how supper was cooked. It became so heated that they slept in separate rooms that night. Neither of them ever approached the other to say, "I'm sorry or to offer forgiveness. Each night they went to bed hoping that the other would approach them with an apology or forgiveness, but it never happened. So, they went on year after year with no forgiveness in sight.

Some might say, "But isn't God's grace and forgiveness free?" Of course, that's correct, God's Grace is free, but it is not cheap. Jesus paid a huge price for our forgiveness. When God's grace comes into our lives, it does not leave us as we were, it changes us. One of the first changes it makes is to give us the power to forgive. By forgiving others we are proving that we have accepted God's forgiveness and are living in it! If we refuse to forgive those who harm us, we are showing that we have not really accepted God's grace, and thus it is removed from us.

Forgiveness has never been hard for me. After all, one who has been forgiven much should be able to forgive much. Hate only hurts the one who hates and what good would it do for me to hate my Mama and Daddy? Even if they knew they were doing wrong, (and I'm not sure they did) I still can't hate them.

Hatred is a dark, selfish emotion that can destroy a human heart in even the best of us. Hatred has a way of taking root within us like no other emotion can. It twists our thinking and causes us to think and do things we would never do, except for hate.

I thank God for removing all hate from me. I can truly say, I love everybody, living and dead. It's a great feeling to love and not hate.

*Mary, Charles, and me with mother shortly before her
death.*

CHAPTER 22

First Miracles of Jesus

As we begin our look at miracles, we want to start with the first miracle of Jesus. It is recorded in the book of John, chapters 2:1–11.

We can't forget the reason John wrote his gospel. He says in John 20:30–31, "Jesus did many other miraculous signs in the presence of his disciples, which are not recorded in this book. But these are written that you may believe that Jesus is the Christ, the Son of God, and that by believing you may have life in his name."

It was John's purpose to encourage people to believe that Jesus is the Christ, the Son of God, and that by believing in Him, one is granted eternal life.

My purpose in writing this book is to encourage people to believe that the same Jesus who performed the miracle of turning the water into wine still performs miracles for his children today.

Jesus and his disciples, along with his mother and many others, were invited to a wedding in Canaan, Galilee. Sometime during the wedding, the wine runs out. We should note that weddings were a big thing during Jesus' time. Sometimes the weddings would last for a week or more. So if you were planning a large wedding, you had better have lots of food and wine on hand.

If you were the one on whom the wedding was depending and you ran out of food or wine, you would be so embarrassed that it would be a disgrace. When this wedding ran out of wine, it was a big thing.

Mary, the mother of Jesus, may have been in charge of the food and wine or may have just been wanting to help. Whatever the reason, she noticed that there was no more wine, and she went to Jesus for help. He tried to explain to her that his time had not yet come, but his mother paid little attention to him and said to the servants, "Do whatever he tells you." Mary must have believed that Jesus could solve the problem. The Bible does not give us any indications of Jesus ever performing any miracles prior to this event. Whatever the reason, Mary, the mother of Jesus, believed Jesus could handle it.

Jesus looked around and saw six stone waterpots, and he instructed the servants to fill them to the brim with water. Now these water pots hold from 20 to 30 gallons of water, and that would be over 120 gallons of water.

The servants did as they were told and brought the water to Jesus. He then told them to draw some out and take them to the master of the banquet. Sometime between the filling of the jars and the headwaiter tasting the water, it had been turned into wine.

To say the least, the headwaiter was shocked; he had never tasted wine so good. He praised the bridegroom for waiting until the end of the wedding to bring out the best wine he had ever tasted.

John states that this is the first of his miraculous signs. Because of this turning the water into wine, the disciples put their faith in him, and from that time on, they knew he was who he said he was.

There are many people who believe that the day of miracles is over and that when Jesus died, so did his work of miracles. Many believe that science has replaced the need for miracles. I don't believe miracles have disappeared, only our ability to recognize a miracle when we see it.

Miracles only happen when we have faith to believe that God will work on our behalf and that there is a willingness on our part to prepare our hearts for them.

MIRACLES

The Filling of a Tooth

The first real miracle I remember as a new Christian was the healing of a toothache. I was in the Air Force and a very new Christian, with very limited knowledge of what being a Christian meant. While attending a Sunday evening service in a little church I had begun attending in Tampa, Florida, I sat suffering from a severe toothache. The pastor, Montez Green, saw something was wrong with me and, after service, came over to where I was seated. She inquired about what was wrong. I told her my problem, and she said, "Well, let's pray about it." She laid her hands on my head and began to pray.

Immediately, the pain was gone. From that day on, I can't ever remember having another toothache.

That was the beginning of my walk in faith about God's ability to perform miracles. Over the many years since that first experience, I have seen God perform many miracles in the lives of my loved ones and myself.

Ring in a Sand Pile

Soon after being engaged to my future wife, Mary Lou, we exchanged class rings. She gave me her high school ring, and I gave her my Air Force ring. I decided to wear her ring on a chain around my neck, but before I could get a chain, I wore it on my little finger. One Saturday, we were playing volleyball with the young people from the church. We were playing in an area filled with sand behind the church. Sometime during that afternoon, I lost Mary Lou's ring; it slipped off sometime during the game. I didn't miss it until that night, and then it was too late to try and find it. I waited until the next day and prayed all the way. I returned to the volleyball court where I had assumed it had been lost. As I arrived, I got out of the car and prayed. Asking God to help me find it, I walked over to where I had been playing the day before, stopped, looked down, and there in the sand was her ring, as if someone had laid it on top of the sand for me to find.

The First Trip to California

The summer after Mary Lou and I were married, we decided to take a trip to California so Mary Lou could meet my mother. We left Florida in my 1956 Ford, praying that I would make it to California and back. It was only a few years old, so we felt we wouldn't have any trouble. When we reached the Sierra Nevada Mountains that ran along the eastern part of California, we began to see steam coming from under the hood. When we pulled over to inspect the situation, we found the hose running from the radiator to the engine had burst and spewed steam all over the place. Here, we were on top of a mountain and had no way of getting any help. We were on a two-lane road with little traffic and didn't know what to do. Mary Lou and I began to pray, asking God for help. I began to walk along the road, just praying and looking, when suddenly I saw a hose down the ditch. I walked down and picked up the hose. It was almost new. I looked it over to see if I could see any holes or breaks in it. There were no breaks or holes, and it was in perfect shape. The only problem I thought of was, will it fit? As I returned to the car, I looked at the one on the car, and it looked like it was made for it. I took the old one off and put the new one on, and it fit like a glove. I noticed a small hole of water in the ditch and was able to fill a bucket and fill the radiator with water. Soon we were on our way again, thanking God for his blessings.

God will make a way even if he has to rain dollar bills down from Heaven.

In 1961, I had just finished my first semester at South-Eastern Bible College, and it was time to pay my school bill. Mary Lou was working at the First National Bank in Tampa, Florida, but her salary was only enough to pay for our normal household bills. It came to the point of either paying my college bill or dropping out. We were very discouraged and had decided I would have to find a job in order to be able to pay the school bill. I had worked for Nichols Mines on a part-time basis during the summer of 1960 and put in an application for summer work again, hoping to be able to save enough money during the summer to pay my bill and continue my schooling.

So it was on a Wednesday night at church that Mary Lou and I had made our decision to drop out for the next semester that the Lord gave us our miracle. During the service, God used an older Christian lady to give a testimony about how the Lord had taken care of her all through her Christian life. Somewhere in the testimony, she made this statement. "God will meet your need, even if he has to rain dollar bills down from heaven." Mary Lou and I both knew the Lord was speaking to us. We went home that night knowing that God was about to perform another miracle for us.

The next day, while I was visiting a friend at his shop, his wife called from their house, telling me I had a phone call. I wondered who would be calling me at my friends' house and how they knew I was there. I answered the phone only to find out it was the personal director for Nichols Mines. He told me he had called my house and was told I was at this number, and I hoped he wasn't bothering me. I said no, he wasn't bothering me, and I was happy to get his call. I was a little disappointed at first, as he started by saying, "I'm sorry, but I don't have any part-time jobs available at this time." As my heart began to sink, he continued and said, "I do have an opening in our laboratory for a full-time opening that starts at 2:00 pm and ends at 10:00 pm. I wonder if you would be interested in that. "

I could hardly keep from shouting as I said, "Yes, I would be very interested." I started the next week, and for the next three years, I worked the perfect job with the perfect hours. My schedule was something like this. I got out of school at 12:00 pm each day with time enough to eat lunch and then drive to Mulberry, Florida, where Nichols Mines was located. My job consisted of driving the company truck to the actual strip mine area and collecting samples for the technicians to analyze the next day. My work was usually finished by about 8:00 each night, which gave me two hours to finish before checking out and heading home. It was a miracle job given to me by God.

Visiting the Indians

My brother-in-law, Alton George, asked me if I would like to take a trip with him and a group of boy scouts to visit an Indian reservation out west. After talking for a few minutes, we decided to visit a missionary we knew from Pleasant Grove, AG, named Barbara Wellard. Barbara was a young lady working with the Indians in Arizona, and it seemed to me we could kill two birds with one stone. We could give the Boy Scouts in his troop the experience of visiting real Indians on the reservation while taking supplies and needed food items to Barbara.

It turned out to be a wonderful trip, just as we had hoped. What we didn't know at the time was that God would have to perform a miracle in order to get us back. We made our journey from Tampa to Window Rock, Arizona, without any real trouble. Alton drove a small van with me and six boys about eight or nine years old. I have always regretted not letting my son Doyle go with us, even though at the time I thought he was too young. We pulled a trailer filled with food and supplies we had gathered from our two churches along with the Pleasant Grove women's ministry. It was wonderful seeing the impact we had on the Indians on the reservation.

Several memorable things happened on that trip that will always be imprinted on my heart. Barbara told us the Indians wanted to give a "feast" to show their appreciation for what we had done. Their idea of a "feast" was to bring a huge pot filled with whatever anyone could spare to put in. It was filled with vegetables of all types and cooked over an open fire for hours. The meat in the soup was to be lamb, given by one of the elders. I watched as the Indian women prepared the lamb to be slaughtered. He was brought to an area to be killed with a large butcher knife. He was turned on his side, and one woman held him down while the other took the knife and began to cut his throat. What made such an impression on me was the fact that the lamb never made a sound, even as his throat was being cut. She had to first cut through the thick wool and then saw into his throat until she had killed him. During the whole time he was being killed, he never made a sound. I was reminded that the Lamb of God, Jesus Christ, was taken as a lamb to the slaughter and not his mouth. Acts 8:32... "He was led like a sheep to the slaughter, and as a lamb before the shearer is silent, so he did not open his mouth."

An Angel at Wolf Creek Pass

As our time of visitation with the Indians drew to an end, we decided to return on a different route than we had come. We packed up the van, said our goodbyes, and headed toward Colorado. In order to return through Colorado, we had to go over Wolf Creek Pass. Being from Florida, where the highest spot in Hillsborough is a hilltop, about twenty feet high, we were not ready for Wolf Creek. As we started up the mountain pass that day, we had no idea what was in store for us. As we began to climb, it began to snow. Slowly, the road began to be covered, and then it really began to snow. It snowed so hard that we could hardly keep it off the windshield. Soon we could not see the road, and then the van began to slow to a crawl. In a few minutes, we were unable to move forward at all. The van then began to slide backwards, and Aldon backed our van off the road onto the shoulder, which was covered with snow, and he finally brought it to a stop. We looked at each other, wondering just what we were going to do now. The snow continued to pile up, and it began to freeze on the outside as well. I don't know how scared the boys were, but I was scared enough for all of us. We began to pray and wondered what we could do. After what seemed like an eternity, we began to see lights slowly moving up the mountain. As we waited and prayed, we were able to make out a large Chevrolet truck. The truck stopped beside us and asked if we needed help. With the snow falling almost as fast as the temperature, we were able to get out of the van, and this man had a chain that he tied to our front bumper and hooked on to his rear bumper, and he began to pull us to the top of that mountain pass. When we reached the top, there was a place to pull off the road and unhook. He said we could make it down now without any trouble. He told us he had been in Mexico for the past two weeks and that he was a dentist from Denver, Colorado, and spent his vacation every year in Mexico treating poor kids. I didn't think for a minute that he was a dentist from Denver. I knew he was an angel sent from God to help two helpless men who needed a miracle.

Give and will be given to you

I had called Mary Lou from the Indian reservation and told her I felt like God wanted us to send Barbara Wellard $75.00 for the Indians. In the early 1960s, we were pastoring a small church, I was teaching at school, and our pay was very little. During the summer, we were not paid at all, and we had to save during the year to make ends meet. We had not budgeted an extra $75.00 in our budget, and we frankly did not have it. But I felt God speaking to me, and when I told Mary Lou, she said, "Well, if God told you to give it, we have to give it." When we returned from our trip, I still felt as though God wanted me to send Barbara the money, so I wrote her a letter telling her how blessed we were for going to visit her, and I also enclosed a check in the amount of $75.00. That morning, I went to the Sydney post office, where we got our mail. I dropped my letter in the outgoing mail slot and then went to my mailbox to get my mail. As I looked through the mail that day, I noticed a letter from our auto insurance company. I opened the letter, and there inside was a letter from the insurance company telling us they were sorry, but they had overcharged us on our premium and was sending us a check for the amount of the overcharge. There in the envelope was a check for $75.00, the exact amount I had just sent Barbara Wellard. I have often thought that the check from the insurance company would not have been in that mailbox if I hadn't first sent the $75.00 check to the Indians.

Doyle's Horse

Often, we wonder if God hears our prayers, but children don't seem to have that trouble. They just pray and believe that God will answer.

One morning, when our son Doyle was about nine or ten, he came in to eat breakfast before going to school. He said to his mother, "Momma, Jesus is going to give me a horse." His mother responded, "Doyle, we don't have any money for a horse." Doyle quickly said, "But mamma, I didn't ask you and Daddy for a horse; I asked Jesus to give me one."

He left for school very excited about soon getting a horse. When he came home from school that day, he was still so excited, and the first thing he said was, "Momma, I had a great day today. Jesus has answered all of my prayers today except one." His mother said, "You mean you asked Jesus for other things today? "," he replied, "Yes, mamma, and He answered them all, except one: I didn't get my horse today." His mother told him to sit down because she wanted to talk to him about prayer. She told him that God always answers our prayers, one way or another. It's just the way he answers: sometimes he says "yes," sometimes he says "no," and sometimes he says "wait." After her explanation, he seemed to be satisfied but still insisted Jesus was going to give him a horse.

Nothing else was said about it until a few days later. We got a phone call from a church member, Johnny Herndon, who, out of the blue, asked us if we wanted a horse.

He said he had a little sandy-colored Arabian mare that belonged to his wife, and she didn't ride anymore. He said it was gentle and would be great for kids. He said he was wondering if we would like to have it for our kids. We told him that we could not afford to buy a horse, and he said, "Why don't you keep her for a few weeks and see if you want her?" If the kids liked her after a few weeks, then we could talk about it. He brought it over and put it in our pasture, and he even brought a saddle and bridle with him.

On our way to church that night, Doyle said, "Daddy, Momma, I just want you to know that Jesus gave me this horse." We could not argue with him. Within a week, Doyle had his horse. God had answered his prayer, even though his mom and dad had their doubts.

Snow in Florida

On January 18, 1977, Doyle, our son, came in and said to his mother and me, "I prayed that it would snow, and God said OK." It was hard to keep from laughing as we explained to him that it does not snow in Florida, but he had faith that Jesus would answer his prayer. We explained that the weather doesn't get cold enough for it to snow. Even though it is rare for snow to fall in Florida, it has happened to a small degree in the past. Freezing temperatures in Florida are caused by cold and dry winds with very little moisture in the air, so it is very rare for any amount of snow to fall in the Tampa Bay area. No matter how much we tried, we could not convince him that it was not going to snow. Mary Lou went on to church for a ladies meeting and told the ladies what Doyle had said. Hilda Swindal, Mary Lou's cousin, said, "Well, I'm going to pray with him."

On that frigid January 19th, 1977, about 5:00 am, we received a phone call from Hilda telling us to get Doyle out of bed and have him go outside. There for the first time in years was Snow. It has not happened in 32 years since, but on that morning, about a half inch of the white stuff fell to the ground. It was not much compared to snowstorms in the north, but it was enough to scrape together a tiny snowman in our front yard. Doyle wasn't surprised because, as he said, "I asked Jesus to let it snow, and he did."

So much havoc was caused by that "snow storm" that almost all the major interstate roads were either closed or at a standstill because of the hundreds of accidents. For Doyle, it was an enchanting introduction to the "white stuff" and again just proved to us that the prayer of a child can be a powerful thing.

The Hannah Fears Story

Suddenly, our lives were shattered! Our only concern had been, would it be a boy or girl? It was a little girl, but in an instant, we were faced with the fact that our little girl might not live.

On December 1, 1991, just before noon, she was born. We had waited for her for nine months, and now the thought of losing her was more than we could bear. "How could such a big baby be so sick?" we thought. She was nine pounds, two ounces, and twenty-three inches long. All day long, we struggled with the thought and the uncertainty of Hanna's condition.

Just before 7:00 PM, the doctors said they had done all they could. Hanna had aspirated meconium and had less than a 20% chance of survival. Dr. Webb, the attending physician, told us there was only one more thing to do. She said ECMO was our only chance, but time was running out and we would have to act fast. None of us had ever heard of ECMO, but we were willing to try anything. We found out later about this new process called ECMO.

ECMO is an acronym for extracorporeal membrane oxygenation. As the name implies, it refers to the delivery of oxygen by "extracorporeal" measures and literally means mechanical bypass that takes place outside of the body. Toward that end, an ECMO machine is a medical device that performs this task. In fact, it is very similar to a heart-lung machine that is used to continue the supply of blood and oxygen while the heart is stopped, such as during open heart surgery. ECMO therapy, however, is intended for patients whose hearts and lungs cannot normally function on their own.

Patients receive ECMO in the intensive care unit of a hospital, where medical personnel specially trained in respiratory therapy can continuously monitor them. The process begins with dispensing an anticoagulant to the patient to minimize clotting of the blood. This is necessary because the patient's blood must pass through a tube to the ECMO machine, where it can be oxygenated by an artificial lung and returned. The machine further simulates human respiration by removing carbon dioxide from the blood. The patient remains placed on the machine until his or her own heart and/or lungs can resume normal functioning. (www.WiseGeek.com)

The one thing we knew was that prayer changes things, and we were praying. Within a short time, the word went out to everyone we could contact to pray for this little girl in Tampa, Florida, who was going to die unless God performed a miracle. Months later, we heard from people all around the United States and as far away as Japan who had prayed for Hanna that day.

At about 3:00 AM on December 2, 1991, we were told we could go into Hanna's room and say goodbye. Dr. Webb had found a hospital with an ECMO machine that had room for her. The only problem was that it was in Atlanta, Georgia, 500 miles away.

After several calls, Dr. Webb found a Medivac airplane in Gainesville, Florida, at Shads Hospital, and they were willing to fly to Tampa and pick up Hanna and fly her to Atlanta. I heard Dr. Webb yelling on the phone in her office and saying, "I don't care how much it costs; put it on my credit card if you have to; just get it here."

Soon, a medical helicopter from Tampa General Hospital came to the Brandon Hospital where Hanna was and flew her to Tampa to await her flight to Atlanta. So, we said goodbye, and Hanna flew off into the dark. We began to prepare for our journey to Atlanta by automobile, but the doctor said not to go because of the chances that Hanna would not make it and they would just bring her body back to Tampa. We waited for what seemed like days, but a little after 7:00 AM, they called and said Hanna had arrived at Egleston Children's Hospital in Atlanta, GA, and was stable after being placed on the ECMO machine.

Over the course of the next four days, Hanna overcame the collapse of one lung and the bleeding of another. The bleeding caused her heart to be pushed over by the amount of blood in her chest. Even with these extra complications, Hanna did better than expected on ECMO.

By Thursday evening, Hanna had progressed to the point where she could be taken off ECMO. On Friday, Hanna was on a jet making her way back to Tampa and on to Brandon Hospital.

Hanna stayed in the NICU at Brandon Hospital for another two weeks. During this time, she was slowly taken off the ventilator and began feeding herself.

Twenty-two days after Hanna was born, with only a 20% chance of survival, she was able to come home, just in time for Christmas.

CHAPTER 23
Reconciliation

I HAVE TO admit, I possessed a tremendous amount of resentment for the greater part of my early years of life. During those days I carried a huge chip on my shoulder and experienced deep frustrations with many people due to the way they had treated me as a child. Many years later, after receiving Christ and experiencing salvation, I realized that anger and bitterness would never serve to accomplish anything positive in my life. For that reason (and with God's help), I set out to reconcile with everyone I felt hostility or resentment against.

After Mary Lou and I were married, we decided to visit my Mama and Daddy who were both living in California, at the time. Daddy lived in Fresno, and Mama lived in Bakersfield, about 100 miles between the two cities. I believe my Mama always felt guilty for leaving her children when she was young, and in her later years she tried to make it up to us. She and Mary Lou became great friends and after a few years, I too became friends with her and forgave her for the past. Daddy, however, was a far different story. It seemed to me that he still only cared about himself. I can't remember him ever going out of his way to make any amends with me or my siblings.

After our son Doyle was born, once again we traveled to California and had an enjoyable visit with Mama and Phil. We decided to drive to Fresno and stay a few days with my brother, Charles. During that trip I heard Daddy was living in Fresno, so I called him and asked him to come over and visit us at Charles' house. He said he was going to Las Vegas to gamble and could only stay for a few minutes (it didn't matter that he had not seen his grandson since his birth).

His visit was anything but pleasant. We barely spoke before we were yelling at each other. I accused him of not even knowing his grandson's name. He shouted, "I know his name, it's Doyle." I yelled, "That's his middle name, what's his first name?" He didn't know, so I yelled, "He was named after you, now do you know it?" At that moment all the anger I had stored up over the years boiled out. I had to restrain myself from hitting him. I wanted to beat him and make him feel the pain I had felt for so many years. At that moment I hated him for everything he had done for me. I blamed him for all the trouble I had gotten into as a boy. I blamed him for divorcing my Mama, for giving me away to strangers, for letting me quit school, for being poor, for all the bad things that happened to me in my short life. If words could kill, he would have been dead there on the ground. He left after a short while, and I didn't see him or hear from him for several years. I knew I couldn't go through life hating my parents, or anyone else for that matter, but I didn't have the opportunity for reconciliation with Daddy until after our third child, Charles Phillip was born.

When Chuck was about twelve years old, we went to Oklahoma to visit my Grandma, and found out that Daddy had supposedly remarried, and moved to Okmulgee to be close to his mother (Grandma Petree). The woman he was living with told me, she and Daddy were married in Mexico, but she never showed me a marriage certificate and I doubt that they ever were married. It was during that visit that I finally had the opportunity to tell my Daddy that I loved him and that I forgave him. He was eager to be reunited with me and we spent several days together reminiscing. As we prepared to leave for home, Daddy asked if Chuck could stay another week with him on the farm where he lived and said he would send him home by air if we would let him stay. Chuck stayed for a week with his grandfather on his little farm, and that visit became one of his best boyhood memories.

I had the pleasure of seeing my Daddy several more times before his death. Though I wasn't there when he died, I knew he had accepted the Lord as his Savior, a short time before. And I know one day I'll see him again. When Daddy was dying of cancer in Okmulgee, I flew to Tulsa and joined my brother, to visit our Daddy in the hospital. We had an opportunity to tell Daddy that we loved him and wanted him to become a Christian. He told us he had accepted the Lord and was ready to die. In that moment all the pent-up anger just seemed to fade away. I was no longer angry with him or even had any bad feelings for him. I just prayed for his healing and hoped he would get well so we could have more time to visit. He died a few weeks later, and I was so glad to have been able to visit with him one more time to share the love of Jesus with him. One of the great things about being a Christian is just to know that this world is not the end. Jesus said to the thief on the cross "Today you will be with me in paradise." I will see Daddy again and we will be able to do a lot of talking when I get to heaven.

Mama and I had reconciled years earlier, and when she passed away, I was at her bedside. She too had accepted the Lord as her Savior. Even though she was Catholic, I heard she confessed her sins and accept Jesus as her Savior while a Nun from her church prayed with her.

We must forgive those who have hurt us, because God commands it, and because our own forgiveness hinges on it. Not only that, but it is also the best thing for us here and now. When we refuse to forgive, bitterness begins to grow within us like a deep-rooted cancer. It eats away our soul. It can cause great stress and even illness. And there is no denying that it saps us of our joy. The only cure for this cancer is the surgical procedure of forgiveness.

As I conclude my story, I want to say that what seemed like a tragic story of loss in my life as a little boy being "given away", ultimately turned out to be a wonderful story of acceptance through the love offered by Jesus Christ my Savior. His work of reconciliation with me came as a direct response to my great need for Him and His great love for me. I will always be grateful for the way God took this little "Okie" from Okmulgee and showed me the depth and breadth of His unending love!

www.ingramcontent.com/pod-product-compliance
Lightning Source LLC
LaVergne TN
LVHW090022070726
842759LV00025B/237